Technical Dynamics

TekDyne
Employee Manual

Karen Iversen
Heald Colleges

Prentice Hall, Upper Saddle River, New Jersey 07458

Library of Congress Cataloging-in-Publication Data

Iversen, Karen S.
    Technical dynamics : TekDyne employee manual / Karen Iversen.
        p.   cm.
    ISBN 0-13-095992-8
    1. Technical education--Case studies.   2. Industrial technicians-
    -Vocational guidance.   I. Title.
    IN PROCESS
    607.1'55--dc21   98-6381
                                                                CIP

Production Editor: *Eileen M. O'Sullivan*
Managing Editor: *Mary Carnis*
Acquisitions Editor: *Elizabeth Sugg*
Director of Manufacturing and Production: *Bruce Johnson*
Manufacturing Manager: *Ed O'Dougherty*
Marketing Manager: *Danny Hoyt*
Editorial Assistant: *Maria Kirk*
Cover Designer: *Marianne Frasco*
Printer/Binder: *Victor Graphics*

©1998 by Heald Colleges
Published by Prentice-Hall, Inc.
Simon & Schuster/A Viacom Company
Upper Saddle River, New Jersey 07458

Printed in the United States of America
10   9   8   7   6   5   4   3   2   1

ISBN 0-13-095992-8

Prentice-Hall International (UK) Limited, *London*
Prentice-Hall of Australia Pty. Limited, *Sydney*
Prentice-Hall Canada Inc., *Toronto*
Prentice-Hall Hispanoamericana, S.A., *Mexico*
Prentice-Hall of India Private Limited, *New Delhi*
Prentice-Hall of Japan, Inc., *Tokyo*
Simon & Schuster Asia Pte. Ltd., *Singapore*

Contents

Acknowledgments

Technical Dynamics was developed and written by
Karen Iversen, Education Department, Heald Colleges

with key contributions by Heald College faculty and staff:
Glenda Allaun
Al Caris
Tom Carter
Gene Coco
Dan Curtis
Diane Cvetic
Dick Dickenson
Lynette Garetz
Monica Goodwin
Steve Harrington
Jerry Hartman
Carol Hicks
Max Jackson
Charles Johnson
Landon Johnson
Francis Ko
Everett Martin
Greg McBride
Walt Nickel
Donald Pierce, Ph.D.
Mike Periclis
Nancy Pope
Ismael Sandoval
Samantha Segale
Paul Shahin
Skip Schaufel
David Scheuermann
Beth Smith
Ted Strahle
Richard Stuart
Vance Venable
David Wilson

To the Student:

Welcome to **TekDyne**. You are about to assume a trainee technician position in a simulated company that mirrors the industry standards and functions of successful businesses everywhere. The difference at **TekDyne** is that experience and prior knowledge are *not* required. At **TekDyne** you will develop the experience, knowledge, interest, inquisitive attitude, and cooperative working skills that will prepare you for future work as a real technician.

This workbook is a series of documents. Some documents are informative, and some involve tasks that are typically performed by employees of a department. For many of the assignments, you and your team members will be challenged to make assumptions, consider alternatives, and develop processes. Think about the materials provided, discuss your thoughts and ideas with your instructor and classmates, and focus your efforts on understanding how and why tasks are organized and completed. Some important tips for getting the most out of your **TekDyne** experience are to:

Articulate your knowledge—by explaining a process or describing a procedure to a team member, you assist that person in developing a clear understanding. More important, such articulation reinforces your own understanding of a concept.

Value your mistakes—mistakes represent opportunities to learn through experience. As a trainee you are expected to make an occasional mistake, and you are expected to learn how and what you did wrong. If you can make mistakes work for you in this way, they can become your most important learning tools.

Seek information—you will be expected to seek information beyond the pages of this workbook and to apply that information in completing tasks. Be creative in this effort now, and you will benefit from the research skills you develop throughout your career. Some clues as to where to seek information are found in the documents. You instructor will provide additional clues. Newspaper and magazine articles, news programs, movies, textbooks, the Internet, and discussions with people who are working in the field of technology will support your knowledge throughout the course.

Karen Iversen
Education Department
Heald Colleges

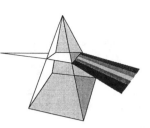

In Basket

Chapter 1
Human Resources

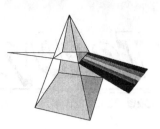

TekDyne
Creating Tomorrow's Solutions Today

One TekDyne Circle, Livermore, CA 94123

Employee Development Program

Welcome to the TekDyne Employee Development Program. This 12-week training program provides an overview of industry standards for customer service, product quality, and workplace expectations. The program also offers career insights and practice in critical thinking activities and team work. The TekDyne emphasis on math, communication, and success skills will support you throughout your career. Those trainees who achieve proficiency in an area will have additional opportunities for supervisory training as they mentor and tutor team members in fundamental concepts.

Employees at TekDyne, as elsewhere in the industry, work efficiently and cooperatively in teams. Changes in team structure and composition present special challenges to individuals, and effective team transition is a valued skill in every workplace. TekDyne emphasizes this skill and maintains a realistic training experience by assigning trainees to new teams in each department.

For the next 12 weeks you will be assigned to various departments at TekDyne and will be required to perform assignments typical of entry-level employees in the industry. Your success is up to you. If you attend daily, complete all assigned activities, and participate fully in team projects, you will maximize your learning power. Your final grade will be determined by the quality of your work performance as judged by yourself, your team members, and your instructor. Remember that initiative and creativity in interpreting assignments and developing solutions are important characteristics of TekDyne employees.

Project Points
Each week your instructor will tell you which activities on the Assignment Log (page 4) your team must complete. You and your team will then divide up the tasks required to complete the assignments and record each person's responsibilities on the Team Task Assignment form, page 5. At the end of the week, when all assignments are due, the team will evaluate each member's performance on the Team Performance Evaluation form, page 6. The team will also decide what percentage of the work each member contributed and select a Team Worker of the Week based on the team evaluation. This outstanding team member earns a 5 percent grade bonus for the module.

Portfolio
At the end of the week, each team submits its portfolio to the instructor for grading. The portfolio should contain the following items:
- One copy of the Assignment Log showing due dates and points possible for each assignment
- A completed Team Task Assignment form for each member
- A completed Team Performance Evaluation form
- Completed assignments as specified on the Assignment Log

At the end of each module, the portfolio should also contain:

- A completed Self-Evaluation and Transfer Report (found at the end of each chapter) for each team member

Your instructor reviews each portfolio for completeness and quality of work, awards weekly grades based on the percentage distribution specified by the team, and returns the portfolio to the team.

Example: *The Technolites team earned 86 out of 100 possible points. The team has four members, so there are 344 points to be shared among them. Based on the performance of the members, the team awarded 35 percent to Greg, 25 percent to James, 25 percent to Jean, and the remaining 15 percent to Henry, who was absent part of the week and unable to contribute much. Since James was selected Team Worker of the Week, he earned a bonus of 5 percent. The team members' individual grades were calculated as follows:*
Greg: 35% x 344 = 120 (Since 100 is the maximum possible score, Greg's grade is 100%)
James: 25% x 344 = 86% + (5% x 86) = 86 + 4 = 90%
Jean: 25% x 344 = 86%
Henry: 15% x 344 = 52%

At the end of the department module, team members assess their own performance and record their points on the Self-Evaluation and Transfer Report found at the end of the module in the *TekDyne Employee Manual*. The completed Self-Evaluation forms are submitted in the team portfolio.

Math Proficiency Exams

Math is a fundamental skill required for success in the technology industry. TekDyne incorporates focused mathematics training for participants in the Employee Development Program. To assess proficiency with the concepts covered, Math Proficiency Exams are conducted in some modules. Record your grade for the exam in the space provided on the Self-Evaluation and Transfer Report.

Final Project

The final project is a written summary of your experience as a trainee for TekDyne. The report should be three to five pages in length, typed double-spaced, and it should address the following issues:

- Review the experience gained in each department.

- Identify the positive and negative aspects of working in each department.

- Identify skills, attitudes, or expectations that you have gained from this course.

- Discuss other changes you have noticed in your work attitude, team participation skills, communication skills, interest and effort, and attention to detail.

- Identify projects and activities that were especially challenging, rewarding, interesting, or surprising.

- Examine your career goals and how this course may have affected them.

- Share any advice you might like to pass on to the next team of trainees.

This report is due at the end of the course, and the subject matter begins today. Keep notes of ideas and thoughts so that you will be ready to complete the final project with time to spare.

Module 1, Human Resources

Trainee: *Your instructor will provide the information necessary to plan your work for the week. Please record this information below for discussion with your team.*

Reading Assignments:
    TekDyne Employee Manual, pages_____

_____

_____

Assignments	Due Date	Maximum Points	Special Instructions
TekDyne Employee Manual **Assignments**			
Interview and Introduction, p. 11			
Employment Paperwork, pp. 13-15			
Dress Standards Task Force, p. 16			
Safety Inspection/Report, pp. 17-18			
Job Descriptions, p. 19			
Additional Assignments			
Total Possible Points This Week:			

Module 1, Human Resources

Team_____   Team Member _____

Performance Expectations: All work is to be thorough, neat, accurate, and completed on time. Teams should assist members in defining outstanding, excellent, satisfactory, and unacceptable performance.

This team member is responsible for completing the following tasks:

Project	Specific Tasks	Special Expectations

Trainee Acceptance of Assignment: I agree to perform the tasks assigned above to the best of my ability and to have my performance on these tasks evaluated constructively by my peers.

Signature: Date:

Team members, please sign below:

_____

_____

_____

Module 1, Human Resources

Team _____

Team Worker of the Week
This team member is recognized for outstanding team support and earns a 5% grade bonus.

As a team, evaluate each member on task performance and on group interaction by checking one line in each column. Be certain that the team agrees on the meanings of each level of performance.

Team Member:	Name		Name		Name		Name	
	Task	Group	Task	Group	Task	Group	Task	Group
Outstanding								
Excellent								
Satisfactory								
Needs Improvement								
Limited Progress								

Grade Distribution
This team agrees that members contributed the following percentages of work this week and will earn the following percentage of the portfolio grade (percentages must total 100%).

Percentage:				
Grade: To be completed by instructor				

Self-Assessment
Use one word to describe your overall rating of your own performance this week. Explain any difference between the team evaluation and your self-assessment in the Comments section below.

My Performance:				
Comment on your attitude, timeliness of work, attendance, punctuality, accuracy, thoroughness, interest, knowledge, equipment proficiency, work habits, appearance, ethics.				
Team Member Signatures:				

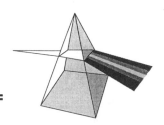

TekDyne
Creating Tomorrow's Solutions Today

One TekDyne Circle, Livermore, CA 94123

Company Profile

Established in 1984, TekDyne is recognized as a leading-edge producer of innovative and precise laboratory test equipment. Ted Kutner, owner and CEO of this dynamic organization, graduated from Heald Institute of Technology in 1965. Immediately following graduation, Ted went to work for a large electronics manufacturing company in Silicon Valley. During the 15 years that Ted worked in Silicon Valley, he became aware of a growing industry need for exacting laboratory test equipment.

It became Ted Kutner's personal goal to design a power supply that would be consistently accurate and reliable. The first step in Ted's action plan was to continue his education. To support that goal, Ted enrolled in evening classes and began working toward an engineering degree. Once his degree was completed, he spent every moment of spare time working on the power supply design that would change his life and would set a new industry standard.

Ted patented his new power supply design in 1984 and began manufacturing on a limited basis from his small Livermore TekDyne plant. When the 1989 earthquake caused a broken gas main and fire destroyed the plant, Ted decided that it was time to seek investors so that he could expand the product line and move into a new facility. A family member, two outside investors, and an attorney eagerly invested in the successful company which Ted Kutner would continue to run.

The Company Today

Today TekDyne manufactures a line of laboratory test equipment including power supplies, analog and digital multimeters, and oscilloscopes. With annual revenues in excess of $45 million, the company employs 180 full-time employees and operates out of an ultra-modern 70,000 square foot glass and steel plant in Livermore, California. The company is notably progressive, operating with a team structure that emphasizes participatory management, quality assurance, and prompt response to market trends.

Ted Kutner recognizes that TekDyne's future success depends on the ability to quickly identify and respond to changes in the market and technology. Each year the company invests over 13 percent of revenue in research and development activities.

TekDyne also supports continued success through its employment practices. Prospective employees are carefully screened and participate in a 12-week training program prior to assignment. Ted frequently returns to Heald Institute of Technology, where he started his career, to hire qualified graduates. He also serves as a member of the Heald Employer Advisory Council and, through his knowledge of the industry, has made important contributions in the development of technical curriculum.

Ted Kutner has built TekDyne to be synonymous with quality, precision, and innovation, and this focused vision has made TekDyne a legend in the industry.

TekDyne

Creating Tomorrow's Solutions Today

One TekDyne Circle, Livermore, CA 94123

Local Organization Chart

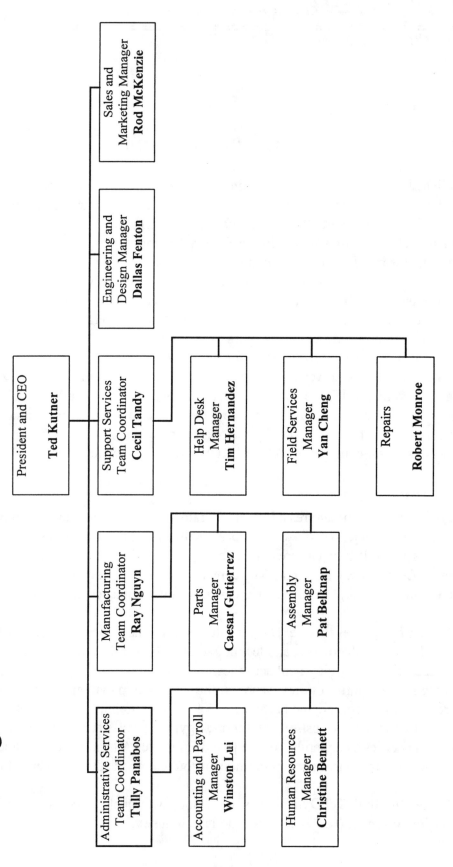

President and CEO
Ted Kutner

Administrative Services Team Coordinator
Tully Panabos

Accounting and Payroll Manager
Winston Lui

Human Resources Manager
Christine Bennett

Manufacturing Team Coordinator
Ray Nguyn

Parts Manager
Caesar Gutierrez

Assembly Manager
Pat Belknap

Support Services Team Coordinator
Cecil Tandy

Help Desk Manager
Tim Hernandez

Field Services Manager
Yan Cheng

Repairs
Robert Monroe

Engineering and Design Manager
Dallas Fenton

Sales and Marketing Manager
Rod McKenzie

TekDyne Guidelines
Working in Teams

TekDyne relies on the creativity and innovative thinking of its employees to solve problems and to generate ideas for new products. Recognizing that the diversity and shared responsibility of a team result in increased levels of efficiency and productivity, TekDyne expects all employees to participate effectively in teams. The following guidelines have been developed to support team members in maximizing their positive interaction.

1. **Make certain that all team members are working toward the same goal.**
Everyone must understand the team's assignment, and all members should assist each other in reaching this understanding.

2. **All team members agree that each member deserves respect for his or her opinions and has the right to explore alternatives and options.**
No one member of the team is always right.

3. **All team members are expected to participate in activities, and all are evaluated on the basis of their participation.**
A team which does not include all its members is like a car running on three wheels.

4. **Individual assignments within a team are as important as the group discussions and explorations which take place.**
Team members are evaluated on their individual contributions as well as their general participation.

5. **Conflicting ideas are sometimes necessary in seeking the best solutions.**
Encourage differing viewpoints and work toward understanding the underlying facts.

6. **Strive for consensus building in team discussions.**
When all members cannot agree on a perfect solution, compromise may result in a solution acceptable to all. Teams do not reach consensus by voting, but by reworking a solution until all members are satisfied.

7. **Rely on concrete facts or information instead of opinion.**
Know the difference between fact and opinion.

8. **Practice listening to other team members and try to understand their positions before insisting that they understand yours.**
Through careful listening, one sometimes learns that what appears to be disagreement is actually accord.

9. **Stay focused on the task at hand.**
A meeting of six technicians at a pay rate of $20 per hour results in a cost of $120 per hour for the meeting. Wasted time is wasted money.

10. **Focus on the issues at hand and not the personalities of team members.**
Disagreements on process or issues can be productive; personal disagreements are counterproductive.

TekDyne
MEMORANDUM

Date: January 25, 19xx

To: New Employees

From: Christine Bennett, Human Resources Manager

Subject: Introductions

Welcome to TekDyne! For the first week of your training program you will be assigned to Human Resources for orientation. During this time you will learn about our facilities, staffing, policies, training opportunities, and benefits. Normally I would introduce you to your training group members on your first day, but I will be in Las Vegas for the annual electronics convention.

Since I cannot be there, please take care of introductions for me. Select another member of your training group as your partner, interview each other, and then introduce your partner to the rest of the group. Important information to share includes:

- Name
- What you hope to learn during training
- What type of job you hope to get after training
- Any special qualifications, including foreign languages, work experience, etc.
- Any other interesting information about you, including special interests or spare time activities

You should spend about 20 minutes interviewing with your partner. Your introductions should each take approximately 1 minute.

Form I-9

U.S. Department of Justice	OMB No. 1115-0136
Immigration and Naturalization Service	Employment Eligibility Verification

Please read instructions carefully before completing this form. The instructions must be available during completion of this form. ANTI-DISCRIMINATION NOTICE. It is illegal to discriminate against work eligible individuals. Employers CANNOT specify which document(s) they will accept from an employee. The refusal to hire an individual because of a future expiration date may also constitute illegal discrimination.

Section 1. Employee Information and Verification. To be completed and signed by employee at the time employment begins

Print Name:	Last	First	Middle Initial	Maiden Name
Address: (Street Name and Number)		Apt. #	Date of Birth (month/day/year)	
City	State	Zip Code	Social Security #	

I am aware that federal law provides for imprisonment and/or fines for false statements or use of false documents in connection with the completion of this form.

I attest, under penalty of perjury, that I am (check one of the following):
☐ A citizen or national of the United States
☐ A Lawful Permanent Resident (Alien # A_____)
☐ An alien authorized to work until ____/____/____
(Alien # or Admission # _____)

Employee's Signature _____   Date (month/day/year) _____

Preparer and/or Translator Certification (To be completed and signed if Section 1 is prepared by a person other than the employee.) I attest, under penalty of perjury, that I have assisted in the completion of this form and that to the best of my knowledge the information is true and correct.

Preparer's/Translator's Signature	Print Name
Address (Street Name and Number, City, State, Zip Code)	Date (month/day/year)

Section 2. Employer Review and Verification. To be completed and signed by employer. Examine one document from List A OR examine one document from List B and one from List C as listed on the reverse of this form and record the title, number and expiration date, if any, of the document(s).

List A	OR	List B	AND	List C
Document title: _____		_____		_____
Issuing authority: _____		_____		_____
Document #: _____		_____		_____
Expiration Date (if any): ___/___/___		___/___/___		___/___/___
Document #: _____				
Expiration Date (if any): ___/___/___				

CERTIFICATION - I attest, under penalty of perjury, that I have examined the document(s) presented by the above-named employee, that the above-listed document(s) appear to be genuine and to relate to the employee named, that the employee began employment on (month/day/year) ____/____/____ and that to the best of my knowledge the employee is eligible to work in the United States. (State employment agencies may omit the date the employee began employment.)

Signature of Employer or Authorized Representative	Print Name	Title
Business or Organization Name Address (Street Name and Number, City, State, Zip Code)		Date (month/day/year)

Section 3. Updating and Reverification. To be completed and signed by employer

A. New Name (if applicable)	B. Date of rehire (month/day/year) (if applicable)

C. If employee's previous grant of work authorization has expired, provide the information below for the document that establishes current employment eligibility.

Document Title: _____   Document #: _____   Expiration Date (if any): ____/____/____

I attest, under penalty of perjury, that to the best of my knowledge, this employee is eligible to work in the United States, and if the employee presented document(s), the document(s) I have examined appear to be genuine and to relate to the individual.

Signature of Employer or Authorized Representative _____   Date (month/day/year) _____

LISTS OF ACCEPTABLE DOCUMENTS

LIST A		LIST B		LIST C
Documents that Establish Both Identity and Employment Eligibility	OR	Documents that Establish Identity	AND	Documents that Establish Employment Eligibility

LIST A — Documents that Establish Both Identity and Employment Eligibility

1. U.S. Passport (unexpired or expired)

2. Certificate of U.S. Citizenship *(INS Form N-560 or N-561)*

3. Certificate of Naturalization *(INS Form N-550 or N-570)*

4. Unexpired foreign passport, with *I-551 stamp or* attached *INS Form I-94* indicating unexpired employment authorization

5. Alien Registration Receipt Card with photograph *(INS Form I-151 or I-551)*

6. Unexpired Temporary Resident Card *(INS Form I-688)*

7. Unexpired Employment Authorization Card *(INS Form I-688A)*

8. Unexpired Reentry Permit *(INS Form I-327)*

9. Unexpired Refugee Travel Document *(INS Form I-571)*

10. Unexpired Employment Authorization Document issued by the INS which contains a photograph *(INS Form I-688B)*

LIST B — Documents that Establish Identity

1. Driver's license or ID card issued by a state or outlying possession of the United States, provided it contains a photograph or information such as name, date of birth, sex, height, eye color, and address

2. ID card issued by federal, state, or local government agencies or entities, provided it contains a photograph or information such as name, date of birth, sex, height, eye color, and address

3. School ID card with a photograph

4. Voter's registration card

5. U.S. Military card or draft record

6. Military dependent's ID card

7. U.S. Coast Guard Merchant Mariner Card

8. Native American tribal document

9. Driver's license issued by a Canadian government authority

For persons under age 18 who are unable to present a document listed above:

10. School record or report card

11. Clinic, doctor, or hospital record

12. Day-care or nursery school record

LIST C — Documents that Establish Employment Eligibility

1. U.S. social security card issued by the Social Security Administration (*other than a card stating it is not valid for employment*)

2. Certification of Birth Abroad issued by the Department of State (*Form FS-545 or Form DS-1350*)

3. Original or certified copy of a birth certificate issued by a state, county, municipal authority or outlying possession of the United States bearing an official seal

4. Native American tribal document

5. U.S. Citizen ID Card (*INS Form I-197*)

6. ID Card for use of Resident Citizen in the United States (*INS Form I-179*)

7. Unexpired employment authorization document issued by the INS (*other than those listed under List A*)

Illustrations of many of these documents appear in Part 8 of the Handbook for Employers (M-274)

Form W-4

Form W-4 (19---)

Want More Money In Your Paycheck?
If you expect to be able to take the earned income credit and a child lives with you, you may be able to have part of the credit added to your take-home pay. For details, get Form W-5 from your employer.

Purpose. Complete Form W-4 so that your employer can withhold the correct amount of Federal income tax from your pay. Form W-4 may be completed electronically, if your employer has an electronic system. Because your tax situation may change, you may want to refigure your withholding each year.
Exemption From Withholding. Read Line 7 of the certificate below to see if you can claim exempt status. *If exempt, only complete lines 1, 2, 3, 4, 7, and sign the form to validate it.* No Federal income tax will be withheld from your pay. Your exemption expires February 17, 19--.

Note: *You cannot claim exemption from withholding if (1) your income exceeds $650 and includes unearned income (e.g., interest and dividends) and (2) another person can claim you as a dependent on their tax return.*
Basic Instructions. If you are not exempt, complete the Personal Allowances Worksheet. Additional worksheets are on page 2 so you can adjust your withholding allowances based on itemized deductions, adjustments to income, or two-earner/two-job situations. Complete all worksheets that apply to your situation. The worksheets will help you figure the number of withholding allowances you are entitled to claim. However, you may claim fewer allowances than this.
Head of Household. Generally, you may claim head of household filing status on your tax return only if you are unmarried and pay more than 50% of the costs of keeping up a home for yourself and your dependent(s) or other qualifying individuals.
Nonwage Income. If you have a large amount of nonwage income, such as interest or dividends, you should consider making estimated tax payments using Form 1040-ES. Otherwise, you may find that you owe additional tax at the end of the year.

Two Earners/Two Jobs. If you have a working spouse or more than one job, figure the total number of allowances you are entitled to claim on all jobs using worksheets from only one W-4. This total should be divided among all jobs. Your withholding will usually be most accurate when all allowances are claimed on the W-4 filed for the highest paying job and zero allowances are claimed for the others.
Check Your Withholding. After your W-4 takes effect, use Pub. 919, Is My Withholding Correct for 19--?, to see how the dollar amount you are having withheld compares to your estimated total annual tax. Get Pub. 919 especially if you used the Two-Earner/Two-Job Worksheet and your earnings exceed $150,000 (Single) or $200,000 (Married). To order Pub. 919, call 1-800-829-3676. Check your telephone directory for the IRS assistance number for further help.
Sign This Form. Form W-4 is not considered valid unless you sign it.

Personal Allowances Worksheet

A Enter "1" for **Yourself** if no one else can claim you as a dependent . . . . A _____

B Enter "1" if { You are single and have only one job; or
You are married, have only one job, and your spouse does not work; or
Your wages from a second job or your spouse's wages (or the total of both) are $1,000 or less. } B _____

C Enter "1" for your **spouse.** But, you may choose to enter -0- if you are married and have either a working spouse of more than one job (this may help you avoid having too little tax withheld) . . . . C _____

D Enter number of **dependents** (other than your spouse or yourself) you will claim on your tax return . . . . D _____

E Enter "1" if you will file as **head of household** on your tax return (see conditions under Head of Household above) . . . E _____

F Enter "1" if you have at least $1,500 of **child or dependent care expenses** for which you plan to claim a credit . . . . F _____

G Add lines A through F and enter total here. Note: This amount may be different from the number of exemptions you claim on your return ▶ G _____

For accuracy, complete all worksheets that apply. {
• If you plan to itemize or claim adjustments to income and want to reduce your withholding, see the Deductions and Adjustments Worksheet on page 2.
• If you are single and have more than one job and your combined earnings from all jobs exceed $32,000 OR if you are married and have a working spouse or more than one job, and the combined earnings from all jobs exceed $55,000, see the Two-Earner/Two-Job Worksheet on page 2 if you want to avoid having too little tax withheld.
• If neither of the above situations applies, stop here and enter the number from line G on line 5 of Form W-4 below.
}

-----------------------------------Cut here and give the certificate to your employer. Keep the top portion for your records.-----------------------------------

Form **W-4**
Department of the Treasury
Internal Revenue Service

Employee's Withholding Allowance Certificate
▶ For Privacy Act and Paperwork Reduction Act Notice, see reverse.

19-

1 Type or print your first name and middle initial	Last name	2 Your social security number

Home address (number and street or rural route)	3 ☐ Single ☐ Married ☐ Married, but withhold at higher Single rate. Note: *If married, but legally separated, or spouse is a nonresident alien, check the Single box.*
City or town, state, and ZIP code	4 If your last name differs from that on your social security card, check here and call 1-800-772-1213 for a new card. . . . . ▶ ☐

5 Total number of allowances you are claiming (from line G above or from the Worksheets on page 2 if they apply) **5**

6 Additional amount, if any, you want withheld from each paycheck **6** $

7 I claim exemption from withholding for 19--, and I certify that I meet BOTH of the following conditions for exemption:
• Last year I had a right to a refund of ALL Federal income tax withheld because I had NO tax liability; AND
This year I expect a refund of ALL Federal income tax withheld because I expect to have NO tax liability.
If you meet all of the above conditions, enter the year effective and "EXEMPT" here **7**

Under penalties of perjury, I certify that I am entitled to the number of withholding allowances claimed on this certificate or entitled to claim exempt status.

Employee's signature ▶ Date ▶ ,19

8 Employer's name and address (Employer: Complete 8 and 10 only if sending to IRS)	9 Office code (optional)	10 Employer identification number

TekDyne

Date: January 25, 19xx

To: Technician Trainees

From: Christine Bennett, Human Resources Manager

Subject: Employee Dress Standards

In a management meeting last week, Mr. Kutner asked that I develop a task force to review our company dress standards. I decided to have your team work on this project because it is an excellent opportunity for you to learn about the importance of dress standards in industry. Please complete each of the following steps.

Step 1
Discuss the communication aspect of appearance and dress, including image, poise, confidence, and first impressions:
- What does the way you dress say about the way you work?
- What is the effect of your appearance on supervisors, customers, colleagues?
- What dress standards do you know of at other companies or schools?
- What is the significance of a uniform?
- Why does a police officer wear a blue uniform, a bus driver wear a brown uniform, and a nurse wear a white uniform?
- What is meant by "dress for success"?
- Which is more appropriate, "over-dressing" or "under-dressing"?

Step 2
Survey three different companies and check with the Director of Career Services to learn what employee dress standards exist in workplaces.

Step 3
Plan a business wardrobe, specifying how many ties, shirts, pants, etc., would be adequate for starting a new job at TekDyne. Include recommendations for styles, fabrics, colors, comfort, durability, and considerations for laundering and hygiene.

Step 4
Using the list developed in Step 3, visit three different stores to price appropriate garments on the list. Include one thrift store, one department store, and one discount store.

Step 5
Present a summary of this information and your recommendations to the department. Teams should model appropriate attire when presenting their reports.

Safety Procedures

TekDyne asks you to cooperate in helping to promote safety and to prevent accidents to yourself, as well as to other trainees, employees, or visitors. No one wants accidents to occur, yet accidents can happen. A little extra care may prevent injuries. Be aware of hazards that may exist. Report them promptly to your supervisor. Be sure you are properly trained to handle any equipment you may need to use. If repairs to facilities or equipment are needed, please report them to your supervisor. To promote the concept of a safe workplace, TekDyne maintains an Injury and Illness Prevention Program. To familiarize yourself with your workplace safety responsibilities, please see your supervisor and ask to review the program which is available in the Human Resources Department. The following ideas may help in keeping TekDyne a safe place to work:

- Keep wastebaskets and machine cords out of walkways.
- If you spill a liquid on a floor, wipe it up immediately.
- Do not run.
- Walk carefully on stairs and always use the handrail.
- Do not overload or put heavy objects on cabinets.
- Do not pull out more than one file drawer at a time.
- Do not leave drawers open and unattended.
- Avoid lifting heavy material; seek help when necessary.
- Learn the TekDyne emergency evacuation procedures and the location of fire alarm boxes and extinguishers.
- Do not operate electrical equipment with wet hands.
- Wear safety goggles when soldering.
- Follow all posted lab safety procedures.

Workers' Compensation (Accident or Injury on the Job)

Workers' Compensation Insurance benefits are available to every employee who is injured on the job. TekDyne pays 100 percent of the cost of this insurance. Every work-related injury which causes a disability lasting longer than the day of the injury or which requires medical services other than first aid treatment is covered by Workers' Compensation Insurance. You should report these injuries immediately to your supervisor, who will see that you receive a claim form and a pamphlet titled "Facts for the Injured Worker." Please give the claim form back to your supervisor. If you must see a doctor or go to the hospital, have the attending physician complete a "Doctor's First Report." All bills relating to the injury can be sent directly to the appropriate Workers' Compensation Insurance company.

TekDyne

Date: January 27, 19xx

To: Technician Trainees

From: Christine Bennett, Human Resources Manager

Subject: Safety Inspection Report

TekDyne conducts regular safety inspections to avoid any safety or health problems that might develop over time. We are due for a safety inspection this week, and it occurred to me that the newest members of the organization would make ideal inspectors.

I have asked your supervisor to assign each team one of the following topics:
- Locations of emergency exits, stairwells, and evacuation maps
- Locations of fire doors, fire alarms, fire extinguishers, and fire escapes
- Potential safety hazards
- Evidence of compliance with safety procedures
- Locations and nature of any posted safety rules

As you conduct your inspection, please try not to disrupt other employees. This is what I would like you to do:

1. With your team, quietly walk through the facility and identify the issues assigned to your team. Take notes on your findings, and record any questions that come to mind during the inspection. Work quickly and return to the department after 15 minutes.

2. Upon completion of the inspection, work with your team members to prepare a map or listing of your findings.

3. Each team will report its findings and recommendations to the department and discuss any additional concerns.

4. Thank you for your help with this project. I think you will find it interesting to explore the facility with your team, and I hope you will be able to describe the advantages of inspecting the facility in teams instead of individually.

Michael Cummings
1862 Spider Lane
Livermore, CA 94123

January 20, 19xx

Human Resources Department
TekDyne
One TekDyne Circle
Livermore, CA 94123

Dear Sir:

I recently completed training in both the Electronics Technology and Computer Technology programs at Heald College and am currently completing the Networking Technology program. In April I will be ready to start work, and I have heard that TekDyne has many excellent opportunities for individuals with my training.

Would you please send me a description of the positions for which you expect to be hiring in the spring. Any information you can provide to assist me in my job search will be appreciated. A copy of my resume is enclosed for your information.

Thank you,

Mike Cummings

Mike Cummings

> *Trainees, would you please collect some classified advertisements or job descriptions for the types of jobs you would like to have after training. We can use them to get ideas for position descriptions for TekDyne jobs. Thanks,*
>
> *CB*

Trainee Self-Evaluation and Transfer Report

Trainee Name	Team Approval	Date	Chapter 1

Performance Record During Human Resources Orientation:

Place a check in the column that best describes your performance in each area:

Area of Training	Outstanding Progress	Shows Improvement	Needs Work
Attitude			
Timeliness of Work			
Attendance/Punctuality			
Accuracy/Thoroughness			
Interest/Team Participation			
Knowledge			
Equipment Proficiency			
Work Habits/Appearance			
Ethics			

Project Points Earned This Department Week 1			
Week 2	NA	Math Proficiency Exam	NA

Comments:

Department Transferred To: **Parts Department**	Start Date:
Instructor Signature	Trainee Signature

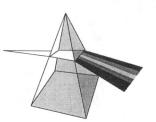

TekDyne
Creating Tomorrow's Solutions Today

One TekDyne Circle, Livermore, CA 94123

In Basket

Chapter 2
Parts Department

TekDyne

TekDyne Guidelines

Position Description and Training Objectives
Parts Department Trainee

Department Profile

The Parts Department, a branch of Manufacturing, maintains and distributes an inventory of all the tools and components used in the manufacture or repair of company products. Employees assigned to this department must identify tools and components, locate sources from which to purchase them, and maintain data regarding usage, prices, and delivery times. Parts personnel analyze production forecasts to estimate projected stock needs, monitor the distribution of parts, and identify special inventory needs. Trainees in this department participate in teams to calculate inventory levels, reorder parts, and assist in developing inventory procedures. Trainees receive ongoing training in math and communication skills, and they participate in the HR achievement program.

Objectives

By the end of the Parts Department module, trainees will:

- Calculate inventory and ordering worksheets.

- Develop a purchasing plan within specified constraints and prepare purchase orders.

- Examine the ethics involved in monitoring inventory usage.

- Participate in team brainstorming as a means to creative problem-solving.

- Write a memo describing a problem and its recommended solution.

- Complete a personal Learning Styles Inventory and identify techniques to maximize learning power.

- Identify color-coded resistors.

- Add, subtract, multiply, and divide fractions in the performance of department activities.

- Self-assess career and training goals and performance in the Parts Department.

Chapter 2 Projects, Parts Department	
• Inventory Losses, p. 28 • Partial Inventory Worksheet, p. 29 • Parts Order Worksheet, p. 32 • Temperature Variations, pp. 33-36 • Purchase Orders, pp. 37-39	• Voltage Calculations, pp. 40-42 • Stock Depletion Report, p. 43 • Defective Stock, p. 45 • Defective Resistors, p. 46 • Resistor Color-Coding, p. 47
Math Proficiency, Parts Department	
No math proficiency exam in this department	

Module 2, Parts Department

Trainee: Your instructor will provide the information necessary to plan your work for the week. Please record this information below for discussion with your team.

Reading Assignments:

    TekDyne Employee Manual, pages_____

_____

_____

Assignments	Due Date	Maximum Points	Special Instructions
TekDyne Employee Manual Assignments			
Additional Assignments			
Total Possible Points This Week:			

Module 2, Parts Department

Team_____   Team Member _____

Performance Expectations: All work is to be thorough, neat, accurate, and completed on time. Teams should assist members in defining outstanding, excellent, satisfactory, and unacceptable performance.

This team member is responsible for completing the following tasks:

Project	Specific Tasks	Special Expectations

Trainee Acceptance of Assignment: I agree to perform the tasks assigned above to the best of my ability and to have my performance on these tasks evaluated constructively by my peers.

Signature: Date:

Team members, please sign below:

_____

_____

_____

Employee Development Program   Team Performance Evaluation

Module 2, Parts Department

Team _____

Team Worker of the Week
This team member is recognized for outstanding team support and earns a 5% grade bonus.

As a team, evaluate each member on task performance and on group interaction by checking one line in each column. Be certain that the team agrees on the meanings of each level of performance.

Team Member:	Name		Name		Name		Name	
	Task	Group	Task	Group	Task	Group	Task	Group
Outstanding								
Excellent								
Satisfactory								
Needs Improvement								
Limited Progress								

Grade Distribution
This team agrees that members contributed the following percentages of work this week and will earn the following percentage of the portfolio grade (percentages must total 100%).

Percentage:				
Grade: To be completed by instructor				

Self-Assessment
Use one word to describe your overall rating of your own performance this week. Explain any difference between the team evaluation and your self-assessment in the Comments section below.

My Performance:				
Comment on your attitude, timeliness of work, attendance, punctuality, accuracy, thoroughness, interest, knowledge, equipment proficiency, work habits, appearance, ethics.				
Team Member Signatures:				

MEMORANDUM

Date: January 31, 19xx

To: Caesar Gutierrez, Parts Department Manager

From: Ray Nguyn, Manufacturing Team Coordinator

Subject: Inventory Losses

The inventory worksheets for the past several months have shown an increase in unaccounted-for inventory. Last month's worksheet indicated a variance between ending balance and physical inventory for 1/8 of the items stocked. This is unacceptable.

Pricing for our products is partly based on the projected cost of components. When parts are unaccounted for, the actual cost of production increases. This increase must then be reflected in our selling price.

Before we begin analyzing selling prices, I think it would make sense to take a close look at inventory control procedures and try to resolve the problem at that level. Effective management of our resources demands that we be able to accurately account for the parts we buy and use.

Please look into this problem and report your findings and recommendations by the end of the week.

> Trainees—
> Please figure out how we can keep better track of inventory. Why do we have missing parts? How can we eliminate the problem? Which items show a variance this month? Why? Please develop a recommended procedure and put it in a memo that I can give to Mr. Nguyn next week. Please check your spelling, grammar, and format.
>   Thanks, CG

Instructions

This worksheet is completed monthly to monitor inventory usage.

Column 1: A brief description of the part.

Column 2: The quantity counted at the last physical inventory.

Column 3: The quantity added during this period.

Column 4: Column 2 plus Column 3.

Column 5: Quantity distributed or signed over to technicians.

Column 6: Column 4 minus Column 5.

Column 7: Quantity counted today.

Column 8: Column 7 minus Column 6. This variance between the *calculated* Ending Balance and the *counted* Physical Inventory represents parts missing and unaccounted for. This number should be zero. Check all calculations prior to reporting a variance.

> *Trainees—I didn't have time to finish this report. Would you please finish it for me and give it to Mr. G. Thanks, pal. I owe you one.*
>
> *Ken Smith, Dept. Clerk*

Column 1	Column 2	Column 3	Column 4	Column 5	Column 6	Column 7	Column 8
Part Description	Beginning Physical Inventory	Added Parts	Total Beginning Balance	Distributed This Month	Ending Balance	Physical Inventory Balance	Variance
Scientific Calculator	12	18	30	24		6	
Breadboard	86	27	115	34		79	
Trimmer Adjustment Tool	162	153	315	181		134	
Screw Driver - Philips	9	25	34	17		17	
Needle-Nose Pliers	23	17	40	15		25	
Diagonal Cutter	18	28	46	32		14	
Wire Stripper	42	0	42	7		15	
Banana Plug to Minihook - Red	35	5	40	8		32	
Banana Plug to Minihook - Black	27	13	40	3		37	
Banana Plug to Banana Plug - Red	38	2	40	12		22	
Banana Plug to Banana Plug - Black	31	9	40	7		33	
10 ft 60/40 Solder	182	163	245	162		183	
2 ft. Solder Wick	76	91	176	43		124	
Soldering Iron Stand	30	10	30	30		5	
Soldering Iron - 25 Watt	55	7	62	48		14	
Printed Circuit Board	67	47	114	52		48	
4-40 Nut	520	800	852	731		73	
4-40 x ½ Aluminum Spacer	116	240	356	206		142	
4-40 x ¾ PHMN	96	134	252	127		103	
9 Volt Battery Clip	93	246	339	234		105	

TekDyne Guidelines
Creative Thinking

**Brainstorming is a team activity that begins with an unstructured
free association of ideas to solve a problem.
There are only a few basic rules:**

1. **Do take risks.**
   Every idea is worth suggesting.

2. **Do listen to the ideas of others.**
   Even if they don't seem like perfect solutions, they might help you think of another idea.

3. **Do borrow from others.**
   It's okay to build or expand on someone else's ideas.

4. **Do think fast.**
   The more ideas the better! It doesn't matter how good or bad the ideas seem.

5. **Do write a list of all ideas generated.**

6. **Do have fun!**

7. **Don't reject an idea.**
   The key is to just get ideas out there, even if they seem impractical and wild.

8. **Don't critique ideas.**
   You can do that later.

9. **Don't be afraid to speak up.**
   Your idea may be better than you think. It might also jog someone else's thinking.

10. **Don't give up.**
    You are a good critical thinker and you probably have at least one more good idea just waiting to be discovered!

Please consult the following information prior to purchasing parts. Careful evaluation of delivery times, prices, discounts, and service ratings can reduce TekDyne product costs.

Part Description and Suppliers	Discount Regular Orders	Service Rating	REGULAR Delivery Time	REGULAR List Price	RUSH Price 1 Week	PRIORITY Price Overnight
Scientific Calculator						
Foster Electronics	5%	Good	4 weeks	32.18	35.26	38.42
Grayline	12%	Poor	6 weeks	38.26	38.26	38.26
Tool Tent	5%	Excellent	2 weeks	31.92	33.05	35.17
Breadboard						
Foster Electronics	5%	Good	4 weeks	4.29	4.82	5.01
Grayline	12%	Poor	6 weeks	3.38	3.63	3.86
Tool Tent	5%	Excellent	2 weeks	3.12	3.12	3.75
Trimmer Adjustment Tool						
Foster Electronics	5%	Good	4 weeks	7.63	7.88	7.95
Grayline	12%	Poor	6 weeks	7.92	8.02	8.26
Tool Tent	5%	Excellent	2 weeks	7.85	7.96	8.06
Screw Driver - Philips						
Foster Electronics	5%	Good	4 weeks	4.26	4.35	4.46
Grayline	12%	Poor	6 weeks	4.26	4.42	4.58
Tool Tent	5%	Excellent	2 weeks	4.09	4.15	4.82
Needle-Nose Pliers						
Foster Electronics	5%	Good	4 weeks	8.31	8.46	8.65
Grayline	12%	Poor	6 weeks	8.05	8.16	8.50
Tool Tent	5%	Excellent	2 weeks	8.63	8.75	9.12
Diagonal Cutter						
Foster Electronics	5%	Good	4 weeks	3.36	3.52	3.68
Grayline	12%	Poor	6 weeks	3.29	3.36	3.52
Tool Tent	5%	Excellent	2 weeks	3.36	3.45	3.56
Wire Stripper						
Foster Electronics	5%	Good	4 weeks	5.28	5.86	6.01
Grayline	12%	Poor	6 weeks	5.63	5.93	6.15
Tool Tent	5%	Excellent	2 weeks	6.29	7.00	7.25
Banana Plug to Minihook - Red						
Foster Electronics	5%	Good	4 weeks	1.96	2.03	2.18
Grayline	12%	Poor	6 weeks	1.79	2.15	2.35
Tool Tent	5%	Excellent	2 weeks	2.05	2.25	2.35
Banana Plug to Minihook - Black						
Foster Electronics	5%	Good	4 weeks	2.12	2.25	2.56
Grayline	12%	Poor	6 weeks	2.23	2.36	2.65
Tool Tent	5%	Excellent	2 weeks	2.24	2.35	2.78

Instructions

Column 1: Description of the part.
Column 2: Physical Inventory from Column 7, Partial Inventory Worksheet.
Column 3: Projected usage per week.
Column 4: Maintain sufficient inventory for 5 weeks usage.
Column 5: Quantity to priority-order for this week's use.
Column 6: Quantity to rush-order for next week's use.
Column 7: Quantity to order for regular delivery.
Column 8: Total parts to order.

> *Trainees, please work in teams to develop your best purchasing plan. Use your good judgment and be prepared to explain your recommendation to the department. When your team is satisfied that your purchasing plan is economically sound and will meet inventory needs, please fill out the purchase orders.*
>
> *C. Gutierrez*

Column 1	Column 2	Column 3	Column 4	Column 5	Column 6	Column 7	Column 8
Part Description	Physical Inventory Balance	Projected Weekly Usage	Minimum Stock Level	PRIORITY Needed This Week	RUSH Needed Next Week	REGULAR Maintain Level	Total Order
Scientific Calculator	6	4					
Breadboard	79	7					
Trimmer Adjustment Tool	134	40					
Screw Driver - Philips	17	6					
Needle-Nose Pliers	25	5					
Diagonal Cutter	14	7					
Wire Stripper	15	5					
Banana Plug to Minihook - Red	32	10					
Banana Plug to Minihook - Black	37	10					
Banana Plug to Banana Plug - Red	22	10					
Banana Plug to Banana Plug - Black	33	10					
10 ft 60/40 Solder	183	50					
2 ft. Solder Wick	124	25					
Soldering Iron Stand	5	3					
Soldering Iron - 25 Watt	14	4					
Printed Circuit Board	48	12					
4-40 Nut	73	200					
4-40 x ½ Aluminum Spacer	142	70					
4-40 x ¾ PHMN	103	40					

TekDyne

MEMORANDUM

Date: January 25, 19xx

To: TekDyne Training Managers

From: Dallas Fenton, Engineering and Design

Subject: Temperature Variations

Engineering and Design is working on a new product that promises a level of accuracy never before attained. This is, needless to say, a challenging prospect requiring a great deal of research.

My technicians are currently trying to determine the effects of temperature on this new product. They have accumulated most of the data, and it needs only to be calculated and analyzed. It will be very helpful if your trainees will calculate the temperature differences listed on the attached pages for us. Once that is done we will be able to make some headway with the project.

Thanks for your help. I will look forward to receiving the calculations by the end of the week.

> *Trainees—*
> *Please calculate the information indicated on the next pages for Mr. Fenton. If you have difficulty, talk to your team members for guidance.*
>
> *CG*

Temperature Variations

Assume the following temperatures in cities across the United States:

City	Temp	City	Temp
Seattle	35°	Chicago	20°
Detroit	–5°	New York	–20°
Washington, DC	0°	Memphis	–10°
Miami	50°	Dallas	30°
Phoenix	70°	Los Angeles	55°

1. What is the temperature difference between Phoenix and Miami?

2. What is the temperature difference between Seattle and Washington, DC?

3. What is the temperature difference between New York and Detroit?

4. What is the temperature difference between Detroit and Los Angeles?

5. Is a temperature of 75° warmer that a temperature of 25°?

6. Is a positive temperature warmer than a negative temperature?

7. Is a temperature of –5° warmer than a temperature of –15°?

8. If a colder temperature is subtracted from a warmer temperature, is the difference higher or lower than the warmer temperature?

9. If a warmer temperature is subtracted from a colder temperature, is the difference higher or lower than the colder temperature?

10. Subtract the temperature in Dallas from the temperature in Los Angeles.

11. Subtract the temperature in Los Angeles from the temperature in Dallas.

12. Subtract the temperature in Chicago from the temperature in Phoenix.

13. Subtract the temperature in Miami from the temperature in Chicago.

14. Subtract the temperature in Washington, DC, from the temperature in Seattle.

15. Subtract the temperature in Miami from the temperature in Washington, DC.

16. Subtract the temperature in New York from the temperature in Dallas.

17. Subtract the temperature in Dallas from the temperature in New York.

18. Subtract the temperature in Los Angeles from the temperature in Detroit.

19. Subtract the temperature in New York from the temperature in Detroit.

20. Subtract the temperature in Detroit from the temperature in Memphis.

21. Subtract the temperature in Memphis from the temperature in Washington, DC.

22. Subtract the temperature in Washington, DC, from the temperature in Chicago.

23. Subtract the temperature in Miami from the temperature in Memphis.

24. What is the average temperature of the cities identified on the chart?

25. Draw a thermometer or number line to graphically illustrate the temperatures given in the chart.

TekDyne
Creating Tomorrow's Solutions Today

One TekDyne Circle, Livermore, CA 94123

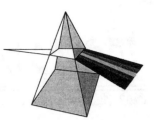

Purchase Order #001368

Date: _____

TO: **Foster Electronics**
      8261 Fremont Avenue
      San Diego, CA

Ship order to TekDyne, One TekDyne Circle, Livermore, CA 94123

Description	Regular Rush Priority	Quantity	Unit Price	Discount*	Total

Total	
Less Discount	
Net	

*Discount applies to regular delivery items only

 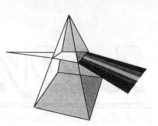

Creating Tomorrow's Solutions Today

One TekDyne Circle, Livermore, CA 94123

Purchase Order #001369

Date: _____

TO: Grayline Electronics Supply Co.
     1900 Madison Way
     San Jose, CA

Ship order to TekDyne, One TekDyne Circle, Livermore, CA 94123

Description	Regular Rush Priority	Quantity	Unit Price	Discount*	Total

Total	
Less Discount	
Net	

***Discount applies to regular delivery items only**

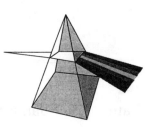

TekDyne
Creating Tomorrow's Solutions Today

One TekDyne Circle, Livermore, CA 94123

Purchase Order #001370

Date: _____

TO: Tool Tent, Inc.
29731 Industrial Drive
Bakersfield, CA

Ship order to TekDyne, One TekDyne Circle, Livermore, CA 94123

Description	Regular Rush Priority	Quantity	Unit Price	Discount*	Total
			Total		
			Less Discount		
			Net		

*Discount applies to regular delivery items only

TekDyne

MEMORANDUM

Date:	January 27, 19xx
To:	TekDyne Training Managers
From:	Robert Monroe, Repairs
Subject:	Voltage Calculations

We have encountered some serious repair issues with the old 286 oscilloscope. We no longer make this product, but the repair department has been overwhelmed with repair requests on the old model.

It is beginning to look like the problems we are encountering might be the result of some inaccurate calculations in the design stage of the 286. The importance of correct calculations cannot be overstated.

It seems to me that this situation actually provides an excellent opportunity for the current trainees to practice calculating voltage differences while providing support in a company crisis. Would you please have them calculate the necessary information on the following pages. The circuit diagram appears on the next page; the requested calculations are on the page following the diagram.

Thanks for your help.

> *Trainees—*
> *Please calculate the voltage differences*
> *indicated on the next pages for Mr. Monroe.*
> *If you have difficulty, talk to your team*
> *members for guidance. It is a good chance for*
> *you to practice a critical skill.*
>
> *CG*

Series-Parallel Circuit
Source Voltage: 9 V

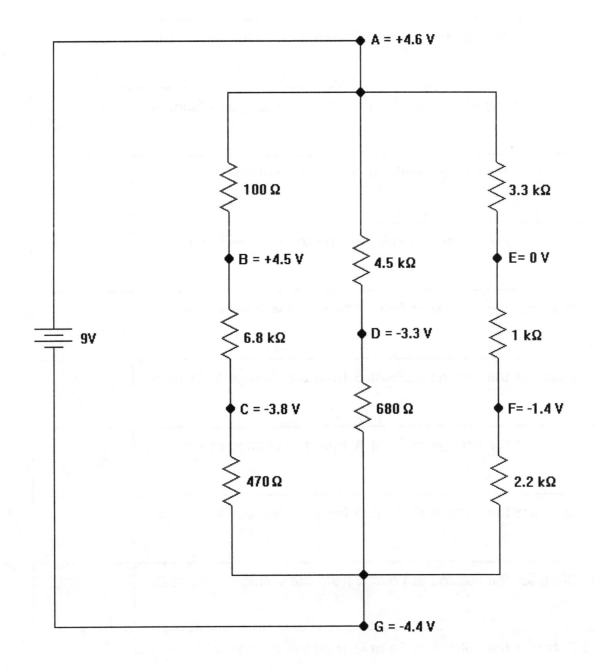

Series-Parallel Circuit
Voltage Differences

Using the circuit diagram on the previous page, calculate the following voltage differences:

1. Subtract the voltage at Point E from the voltage at Point B.	
2. Subtract the voltage at Point B from the voltage at Point A.	
3. Subtract the voltage at Point D from the voltage at Point E.	
4. Subtract the voltage at Point F from the voltage at Point C.	
5. Subtract the voltage at Point B from the voltage at Point F.	
6. Subtract the voltage at Point G from the voltage at Point A.	
7. Subtract the voltage at Point A from the voltage at Point G.	
8. Subtract the voltage at Point D from the voltage at Point F.	
9. Subtract the voltage at Point E from the voltage at Point C.	
10. Subtract the voltage at Point G from the voltage at Point E.	

TekDyne
MEMORANDUM

Date: February 18, 19xx

To: Ray Nguyn, Manufacturing Team Coordinator

From: Caesar Gutierrez, Parts Department Manager

Subject: Stock Depletion Report for January

Trainees, please complete columns 7 and 8 and then give this report to Mr. Nguyn.

Thanks,

CG

Last month you asked that we keep a record to indicate what fraction of stock is used each week so that we could determine how close our actual depletion is to 1/5 of the inventory each week. The following report provides that information.

Column 1 Part Description	Column 2 Beginning Inventory Level	Column 3 Fraction Used Week 1	Column 4 Fraction Used Week 2	Column 5 Fraction Used Week 3	Column 6 Fraction Used Week 4	Column 7 Fraction Remaining	Column 8 No. Parts Remaining
Scientific Calculator	20	3/20	1/4	1/5	3/10		
Breadboard	35	1/5	8/35	6/35	2/7		
Trimmer Adjustment Tool	200	1/4	1/5	3/10	3/20		
Screw Driver - Philips	30	1/6	1/5	2/15	1/10		
Needle-Nose Pliers	25	4/25	1/5	6/25	3/25		
Diagonal Cutter	35	6/35	1/5	8/35	1/7		
Wire Stripper	25	1/5	4/25	1/5	6/25		
Banana Plug to Minihook - Red	50	4/25	1/5	9/50	6/25		
Banana Plug to Minihook - Black	50	1/25	6/25	1/5	3/25		
Banana Plug to Banana Plug - Red	50	3/25	6/25	1/5	4/25		
Banana Plug to Banana Plug - Black	50	1/5	7/25	2/25	11/50		
10 ft 60/40 Solder	350	12/175	3/25	2/25	11/175		
2 ft. Solder Wick	125	26/125	24/125	4/25	23/125		
Soldering Iron Stand	15	1/5	0/0	1/15	4/15		
Soldering Iron - 25 Watt	20	1/4	1/10	1/5	3/20		
Printed Circuit Board	60	1/4	1/5	17/60	1/6		
4-40 Nut	1000	3/20	1/4	1/5	7/40		
4-40 x ½ Aluminum Spacer	350	13/70	71/350	6/35	3/14		
4-40 x ¾ PHMN	200	9/40	1/4	4/25	41/200		
9 Volt Battery Clip	325	12/65	13/65	14/65	56/325		

Resistor Color Codes

The purpose of all fixed resistors is to control or reduce current that is generated from the power source.

The resistor color code is used to identify resistance values in ohms (Ω), kilohms (KΩ), and megohms (MΩ). The resistor color code usually consists of four or five color bands on the outside of the resistor. Each color represents a number as shown in the resistor color codes chart.

Resistor Color Codes				
Color	Band 1	Band 2	Band 3 (if used)	Multiplier	Tolerance
	First Digit	Second Digit	Third Digit		
Black	0	0	0	1	
Brown	1	1	1	10	±1%
Red	2	2	2	100	±2%
Orange	3	3	3	1,000	
Yellow	4	4	4	10,000	
Green	5	5	5	100,000	
Blue	6	6	6	1,000,000	
Violet	7	7	7	10,000,000	
Grey	8	8	8		
White	9	9	9		
Gold				0.1	±5%
Silver				0.01	±10%
No Color					±20%

TekDyne

MEMORANDUM

Date: February 23, 19xx

To: Parts Department

From: Jim Rose, Accounting Department

Subject: Defective Stock

Grayline Electronics Supply Company called today to apologize for the defective stock they sent last month. They asked that we pay them only a fraction of the amount they billed us, but I do not understand how to calculate the amount to pay. Since you are more familiar with the situation, I would like to stop by tomorrow and have you explain how I can calculate the amount to pay Grayline. This is the information they gave me:

112 of the 500 1 KΩ resistors *were defective.* *We were billed $395.00.*

36 of the 172 3.3 KΩ resistors *were defective.* *We were billed $29.00.*

71 of the 150 6.8 KΩ resistors *were defective.* *We were billed $26.00.*

97 of the 125 10 KΩ resistors *were defective.* *We were billed $23.00.*

22 of the 48 100 KΩ resistors *were defective.* *We were billed $12.00.*

236 of the 300 910 KΩ resistors *were defective.* *We were billed $79.00.*

We should pay only for the good resistors.

Thanks for your help. I look forward to talking with you tomorrow.

TekDyne

Date: February 24, 19xx

To: Parts Department Trainees

From: Robert Monroe, Repair Department

Subject: Defective Resistors

We believe that some of the resistors we recently received from Grayline Electronics are not within tolerance and therefore not suitable for stocking. We plan to have staff in the repair department measure the actual resistances of the suspect resistors to determine if they can be used. To help them determine if the resistors are useable, please fill in the table below to show the minimum and maximum resistances acceptable for each of the types of resistors shown.

Tolerance	1%		5%		10%	
Resistance	Minimum	Maximum	Minimum	Maximum	Minimum	Maximum
100 Ω						
4.7K Ω						
10K Ω						
120K Ω						
2M Ω						

We just received another batch of resistors from Grayline, and this time they have *no* color coding! They arrived in an order of **100Ω, 1KΩ, 6.8KΩ, and 100KΩ resistors**, so each must be one of those.

The measured resistances are identified below, and I have already determined the proper value and color coding for the first one. Would you please do the same for the others listed.

Thanks,

CG

Resistance (Ohms)	Resistor (Ohms)	Tolerance
104	100	5%
113		
118		
121		
123		
913		
956		
987		
999		
1042		
1075		
1084		
1115		
1124		
1142		
1194		
4834		
5091		
5601		

Resistance (Ohms)	Resistor (Ohms)	Tolerance
5713		
6046		
6691		
7460		
7626		
7774		
7979		
8019		
80275		
83395		
84609		
88665		
103208		
104533		
105597		
108647		
108844		
109419		
110660		

Trainee Self-Evaluation and Transfer Report

Trainee Name	Team Approval	Date	Chapter
			2

Performance Record in Parts Department:

Place a check in the column that best describes your performance in each area:

Area of Training	Outstanding Progress	Shows Improvement	Needs Work
Attitude			
Timeliness of Work			
Attendance/Punctuality			
Accuracy/Thoroughness			
Interest/Team Participation			
Knowledge			
Equipment Proficiency			
Work Habits/Appearance			
Ethics			

Project Points Earned This Department Week 1			
Week 2	NA	Math Proficiency Exam	NA

Comments:

Department Transferred To: **Assembly Department**	Start Date:
Instructor Signature	Trainee Signature

Creating Tomorrow's Solutions Today

One TekDyne Circle, Livermore, CA 94123

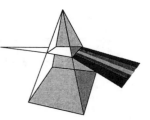

In Basket

Chapter 3
Assembly Department

51

TekDyne Guidelines
Position Description and Training Objectives
Assembly Department Trainee

Department Profile

The Assembly Department, a branch of Manufacturing, is where the components of a company product are assembled to produce the complete unit. After the Engineering and Design department designs a new product and builds a prototype, documentation specifies exactly what parts and tools are necessary, schematics are drawn up, and Assembly employees begin the job of actually building the product. Assembly personnel also monitor quality control of parts, tools, and final products, and develop standards for productivity. Trainees in this department participate in teams to document quality control and productivity, participate in a special training workshop to learn safe and effective soldering techniques, and assemble products using established guidelines. Trainees continue math, communication, and achievement training during their two-week assignment to Assembly.

Objectives

By the end of the Assembly Department module, trainees will:

- Describe and demonstrate safe and effective soldering and de-soldering techniques.
- Identify and correct defective soldering connections.
- Participate in team problem solving to develop quality control standards and systems.
- Define and prioritize team and department goals.
- Write a memorandum outlining an improvement plan.
- Plot a graph depicting current and projected rejection rates.
- Add, subtract, multiply, and divide decimal numbers and convert fractions to decimals and percentages in the performance of department activities.
- Calculate Quality Exception Report and rejection rate.
- Calculate Employee Time Sheet and production per hour.
- Calculate Daily Production by Shift and determine rejection ratios for shift personnel.
- Analyze productivity and quality measurement reports.
- Assemble and test a European siren kit.
- Measure acceptance rate for production.
- Use a problem-solving model to support critical thinking.

Chapter 3 Projects, Assembly Department	
• Quality Assurance, p. 59	• Weekly Productivity Summary, p. 76
• Soldering Exercises 1-4, pp. 68-72	• Product #427, p. 77
• Quality Exception Report, p. 73	• Problem Solving Model, pp. 79-81
• Employee Time and Prod. Record, p. 74	• Stock Depletion Report, pp. 82-83
• Daily Production by Shift, p. 75	• Quality Inspection Report, p. 84
Math Proficiency, Assembly Department	
Exam #1: The Decimal Number System	

Module 3-1, Assembly Department

Trainee: Your instructor will provide the information necessary to plan your work for the week. Please record this information below for discussion with your team.

Reading Assignments:

    TekDyne Employee Manual, pages_____

    _____

    _____

Assignments	Due Date	Maximum Points	Special Instructions
TekDyne Employee Manual Assignments			
Additional Assignments			
Total Possible Points This Week:			

Module 3-2, Assembly Department

Trainee: *Your instructor will provide the information necessary to plan your work for the week. Please record this information below for discussion with your team.*

Reading Assignments:
   TekDyne Employee Manual, pages_____
   _____
   _____

Assignments	Due Date	Maximum Points	Special Instructions
TekDyne Employee Manual Assignments			
Additional Assignments			
Total Possible Points This Week:			

Module 3-1, Assembly Department

Team_____   Team Member _____

Performance Expectations: All work is to be thorough, neat, accurate, and completed on time. Teams should assist members in defining outstanding, excellent, satisfactory, and unacceptable performance.

This team member is responsible for completing the following tasks:

Project	Specific Tasks	Special Expectations

Trainee Acceptance of Assignment: I agree to perform the tasks assigned above to the best of my ability and to have my performance on these tasks evaluated constructively by my peers.

Signature: Date:

Team members, please sign below:

_____

_____

_____

Module 3-2, Assembly Department

Team_____   Team Member _____

Performance Expectations: All work is to be thorough, neat, accurate, and completed on time. Teams should assist members in defining outstanding, excellent, satisfactory, and unacceptable performance.

This team member is responsible for completing the following tasks:

Project	Specific Tasks	Special Expectations

Trainee Acceptance of Assignment: I agree to perform the tasks assigned above to the best of my ability and to have my performance on these tasks evaluated constructively by my peers.

Signature: Date:

Team members, please sign below:

_____

_____

_____

Module 3-1, Assembly Department

Team _____

Team Worker of the Week
This team member is recognized for outstanding team
support and earns a 5% grade bonus.

As a team, evaluate each member on task performance and on group interaction by checking one line in each column. Be certain that the team agrees on the meanings of each level of performance.

Team Member:	Name		Name		Name		Name	
	Task	Group	Task	Group	Task	Group	Task	Group
Outstanding								
Excellent								
Satisfactory								
Needs Improvement								
Limited Progress								

Grade Distribution
This team agrees that members contributed the following percentages of work this week and will earn the following percentage of the portfolio grade (percentages must total 100%).

Percentage:				
Grade: To be completed by instructor				

Self-Assessment
Use one word to describe your overall rating of your own performance this week. Explain any difference between the team evaluation and your self-assessment in the Comments section below.

My Performance:				
Comment on your attitude, timeliness of work, attendance, punctuality, accuracy, thoroughness, interest, knowledge, equipment proficiency, work habits, appearance, ethics.				
Team Member Signatures:				

Employee Development Program   Team Performance Evaluation

Module 3-2, Assembly Department

Team _____

Team Worker of the Week
This team member is recognized for outstanding team
support and earns a 5% grade bonus.

As a team, evaluate each member on task performance and on group interaction by checking one line in each column. Be certain that the team agrees on the meanings of each level of performance.

Team Member:	Name		Name		Name		Name	
	Task	Group	Task	Group	Task	Group	Task	Group
Outstanding								
Excellent								
Satisfactory								
Needs Improvement								
Limited Progress								

Grade Distribution
This team agrees that members contributed the following percentages of work this week and will earn the following percentage of the portfolio grade (percentages must total 100%).

Percentage:				
Grade: To be completed by instructor				

Self-Assessment
Use one word to describe your overall rating of your own performance this week. Explain any difference between the team evaluation and your self-assessment in the Comments section below.

My Performance:				
Comment on your attitude, timeliness of work, attendance, punctuality, accuracy, thoroughness, interest, knowledge, equipment proficiency, work habits, appearance, ethics.				
Team Member Signatures:				

TekDyne
MEMORANDUM

Date: February 28, 19xx

To: Pat Belknap, Assembly Department Manager

From: Ray Nguyn, Manufacturing Team Coordinator

Subject: Quality Assurance

Pat, I am concerned that our assembly rejection rate is out of line. Last year at this time we rejected .05 of all units built. Last month our rejection rate was .213. This is very difficult to justify and requires a close look at our quality assurance procedures. Our cost per unit budgeting is ineffective when defective units exceed the anticipated range. Unless we can reduce the rejection rate, it will be necessary to increase the estimated cost-per-unit, and that increase will then be passed on to our customers. I would prefer to keep our customers happy and increase quality production rather than price.

You are starting a new group of trainees today, and I would like you to do the following:

1. Emphasize the importance of practicing soldering until each trainee has mastered the art. Poor soldering connections are a frequent cause of defective units.
2. Emphasize the importance of following safety procedures to avoid damage to personnel, equipment, and completed units. Injured employees and damaged equipment and materials are costly results.
3. Review the quality control standards currently in place. These standards must be met during production to ensure that completed units will not be defective.
4. Have the trainees work together to find ways to INCREASE our acceptance rate and our overall quality and productivity. Highly skilled and motivated team players take pride in doing their jobs well.

I observed this group of trainees as they worked in the Parts Department, and they are a fine group of individuals. I am confident that they will be able to improve your department operations.

> *Trainees—*
> *As you can see, Mr. Nguyn has a great deal of confidence in you! Welcome to the department. I hope you will enjoy working here and that you will begin seeking ways to improve this department's performance. Please brainstorm with your team to develop a plan to improve our acceptance rate, and describe your plan in a memo to Mr. Nguyn.   PB*

TekDyne Guidelines
Lab Safety Procedures

The following lab safety guidelines have been developed to ensure a safe working environment for you and your co-workers. All employees are required to follow these procedures. Failure to do so may result in disciplinary action up to and including termination.

1. Wear safety goggles when working with solder.

2. Place a protective board on the lab table top to prevent damage while soldering.

3. Soldering irons reach temperatures between 500°F and 700°F. Be extremely careful when handling the iron. *Always* place the iron in its stand when not in use.

4. Do not allow the tip of the soldering iron to touch the soldering iron stand. This could cause the soldering iron to generate excess heat (thermal run-away) that could destroy the soldering iron.

5. Do not inhale fumes that rise from soldering. Though non-toxic, they do contain flux, oxides, and lead.

6. Take care when moistening the soldering-stand sponge with water. The sponge should be wet enough that water can be squeezed from it; it should **not** be soaking wet. Have paper towels available to wipe up any excess water.

7. Before soldering, clear the table of anything that is not needed for the immediate project.

The Basics

Proper operation requires well-soldered connections. It takes as much time and effort to solder a connection poorly as it does to make a good soldering connection.

Solder
The 60/40 solder used in this department contains 60 percent tin, 40 percent lead, and rosin-core flux. The flux removes any oxides from the metal.

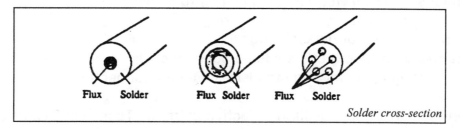

Solder cross-section

Oxidation
Tin the soldering iron before and after soldering to prevent oxides from forming on the tip of the soldering iron. When not in use, the soldering iron should always have a thin coat of solder on the tip to protect it from oxidizing. If an oxidizing layer is formed on the tip of the soldering iron, the iron will not heat enough to melt the solder. If the soldering iron tip does become oxidized, attempt to remove the oxidation with steel wool. If steel wool does not remove the oxidation, the soldering iron tip will not heat properly and must be replaced.

Tinning
Tin the soldering iron by melting a small amount of solder onto the soldering iron tip. Also tin the area to be soldered; e.g., if two leads are going to be soldered together, tin each lead first. When tinning stranded wire, the form of the individual wire strands should still be visible after tinning.

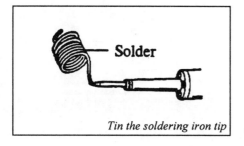

Tin the soldering iron tip

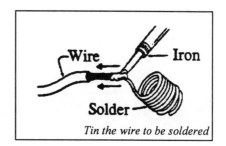

Tin the wire to be soldered

The Soldering Process

A soldering iron heats the connection so that the solder melts when it contacts the connection. A soldering iron is ***not*** meant to melt the solder.

Meeting Quality Standards

The next several pages of this employee manual describe:

- Terms and abbreviations relevant to soldering
- Preparations to be taken prior to beginning to solder
- Seven-step technique for correct soldering
- Five-step technique for de-soldering
- Characteristics of a correctly soldered connection
- Troubleshooting chart for sub-standard soldering connections

Since poor soldering connections result in defective units, all Technical Dynamics employees are required to practice soldering techniques before beginning any assembly work.

Terms and Abbreviations

LED:	Light emitting diode. Diodes are polarized.
Soldering:	The process of connecting two metal conductors.
60/40 solder:	A conductive metal made of 60 percent tin and 40 percent lead.
Alloy:	Tin and lead chemically combined to form solder.
De-solder:	Remove solder from a soldered component.
Solder wick:	A very porous copper braid used to de-solder components.
PCB:	Printed circuit board.
Solder side:	Copper side of the PCB.
Component side:	Non-copper side of the PCB.
22 gauge:	Measurement to indicate the thickness of wire.
PHMS:	Philips-head metal screw.
NOPB:	Normally-open push button.
SPST:	Single pole, single throw.
SPDT:	Single pole, double throw.
Protoboard:	Board enables circuits to be connected without soldering.
Insulation:	Material that does not allow current to pass.
Oxide:	Thin insulator created as solder is exposed to air.
Flux:	Non-corrosive cleaning agent used to remove oxides from metal.
Rosin-core:	A type of flux contained within the solder.
Tinning:	Process of applying a layer of solder to a surface.
Void:	An area on a component or board that should have been soldered.
Solder bridge:	An unwanted soldering connection.
Stranded wire:	Individual lengths of thin wire twisted together to form a single wire.
Wetting:	Process of embedding the solder in the metal.
Trace:	A built-in conductor found on a printed circuit board.
Lead:	The conductive ends of any component.
Lug:	Metal terminal to which wires are fastened prior to soldering.

Work Station Preparation

1. Place a protective board on the lab table top to prevent damage while soldering.

2. Assemble the soldering iron stand as illustrated.

3. Plug in the soldering iron and place the iron in the soldering iron stand. Do not allow the tip of the soldering iron to touch the soldering iron stand. This could cause the soldering iron to generate excess heat (thermal run-away) that could destroy the soldering iron. After a minute or so the tip of the soldering iron will start smoking. This smoke was the protective coating put on at the manufacturing plant. The coating keeps the soldering iron tip from oxidizing.

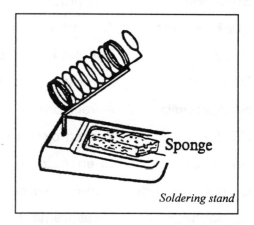

Sponge

Soldering stand

4. While the soldering iron is heating up, moisten the soldering-stand sponge with water. The sponge should be wet enough that water can be squeezed from it; it should not be soaking wet. Use paper towels to wipe up any excess water.

5. Assemble all required materials. Remove any unnecessary items from the lab table to allow more space and to prevent accidents.

Seven-Step Soldering Procedure:

1. Clean the tip of the soldering iron on a damp sponge.

Clean the tip

2. Tin the tip of the soldering iron, and tin the area to be soldered.
3. Heat the connection for 1 to 3 seconds.

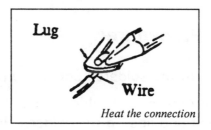

Heat the connection

4. Apply the solder to the opposite side of the connection. When soldering, hold the soldering iron at a 45° angle.

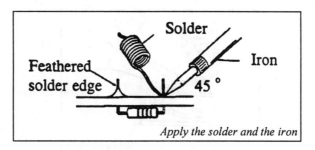

Apply the solder and the iron

5. Leave the tip of the soldering iron on the connection only long enough to melt the solder. One to two seconds is generally enough time.

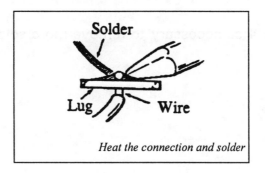

Heat the connection and solder

6. Remove the solder and then the iron. Do **not** disturb the solder while it is solidifying. As the solder solidifies, it actually penetrates into the metals. This is called *wetting*.

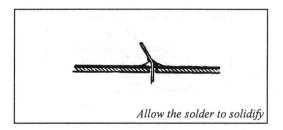

Allow the solder to solidify

6. Re-tin the tip of the soldering iron before placing it in the soldering iron stand.

Five-Step De-Soldering Procedure:

1. Place the solder wick on top of the soldered connection.

2. Place the soldering iron tip on top of the solder wick. As the solder wick heats, it transfers enough heat to melt and absorb the solder. Hold the solder wick several inches from the connection to avoid burned fingers; heat travels quickly through the wick.

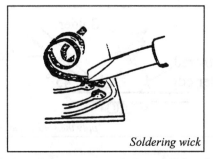

Soldering wick

3. Remove the iron and the wick when most of the solder has been removed.

4. Allow the wick to cool and use the diagonal cutters to cut off the used portion of the wick.

5. Repeat Steps 1 through 4 as necessary to remove more solder.

Characteristics of High Quality Soldering:

A high quality soldering connection shows the following characteristics:

- *The connection is smooth and shiny.*
- *The solder feathers out to a thin edge.*

Troubleshooting Sub-Standard Soldering Connections:

A poor quality soldering connection is one of the following:

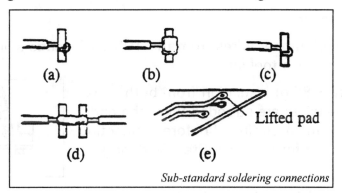

Sub-standard soldering connections

Problem	Characteristics/Cause	Remedy/Prevention
a) Cold solder joint	The connection has a dull gray appearance. It is caused by lead movement before the solder cooled or by not heating the connection enough before soldering.	Re-solder the connection.
b) Excessive solder joint	This connection is caused by applying too much solder or by using solder that is too thick.	Remove excess solder using the solder wick.
c) Insufficient solder joint	This connection occurs when not enough solder is applied. It is sometimes referred to as a *void*.	Re-solder the connection.
d) Solder bridge	This connection occurs when two closely situated electrical paths are soldered together. It is usually caused by too much solder.	Remove excess solder using the solder wick.
e) Excessive heat	If too much heat is used on a printed circuit board, it could cause a trace or pad to lift. It is usually caused by leaving the soldering iron on the board too long.	Prevent this by holding the soldering iron on the connection for only 1 to 2 seconds.

Training Exercise 1: Soldering Jumper Wires

In this exercise, trainees practice soldering skills by soldering and de-soldering individual jumper wires.

Materials Required:
- Soldering iron, stand, wet sponge, paper towel
- 60/40 alloy solder
- Solder wick

- 22 gauge solid core wire
- Needle-nose pliers
- Diagonal cutters
- Wire strippers

1. Prepare the work station.

2. Cut two 3" lengths of jumper wires from the 10 ft. 22-gauge solid core wire included in the Technical Dynamics tool kit.

3. Strip approximately 3/8" of insulation from both ends of each wire. If the wires are stranded wire, the end of the stranded wire must be tinned before connecting the wires together. (Refer to Seven-Step Soldering Procedure.)

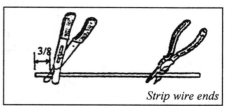
Strip wire ends

4. Use the needle nose pliers to form a hook in one end of each wire.

5. Connect the two hooks together as illustrated in Figure 13. Make sure the connection between the hooks is secure. If they are too loose, they could move during soldering, causing a cold solder joint.

6. Solder the two wires together by following the "Seven-Step Soldering Procedure."

Connect the hooked wires

7. Check for quality: A good solder joint is identified by a smooth, shiny surface. At the connection each individual hook should be clearly visible through the solder.

8. Check for quality: Hold the wire by the ends and bend it into the shape of a "U." If the soldering is good, the bend does not occur at the soldered joint.

9. Check for quality: Have a team member assess the quality of the soldered connection.

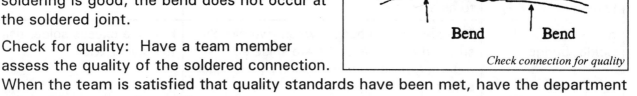
Bend   **Bend**
Check connection for quality

When the team is satisfied that quality standards have been met, have the department supervisor assess for quality.

Training Exercise 2: De-Soldering Jumper Wires

In this exercise, trainees practice de-soldering skills by de-soldering the jumper wires soldered in Training Exercise 1.

Materials Required:
- Soldering iron, stand, wet sponge, paper towel
- Solder wick
- Needle-nose pliers
- Diagonal cutters
- Soldered wires from Training Exercise 1.

1. De-solder the two wires by following the "Five-Step De-Soldering Procedure."

2. Check for quality: While not all of the solder can be removed, enough should be removed to allow the two hooks to be disconnected by using needle-nose pliers.

Training Exercise 3: Soldering and De-Soldering Jumper Wires on a Printed Circuit Board

In this exercise, trainees practice soldering skills by soldering jumper wires on a printed circuit board. Use the same jumper wires used in Exercises 1 and 2, or cut new wires.

Materials Required:
- Soldering iron, stand, wet sponge, paper towel
- 60/40 alloy solder
- Solder wick
- 22 gauge solid core wire
- Printed circuit board

- 4 4-40 nuts
- 4 4-40 x ½" aluminum spacers
- 4 4-40 x ¾" PHMS
- Needle-nose pliers
- Diagonal cutters
- Wire strippers

1. To simplify soldering, mount "legs" formed by nuts, spacers, and PHMS at each corner of the PCB.

   The solder side (copper side) of the PCB is on the top, and the component side (non-copper side) is on the bottom.

   Any component is inserted on the PCB from the component side of the board.

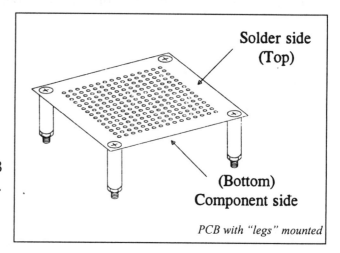

Solder side (Top)

(Bottom) Component side

PCB with "legs" mounted

2. Insert the two jumper wires on the PCB.

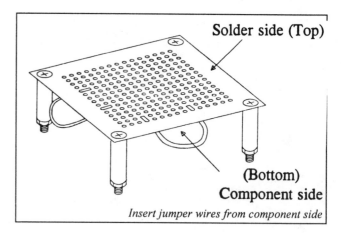

Solder side (Top)

(Bottom) Component side

Insert jumper wires from component side

3. Bend the wires sticking out of the solder side of the PCB.

   This will hold the jumper wires in place during soldering. A typical example using components is illustrated in Figure 17.

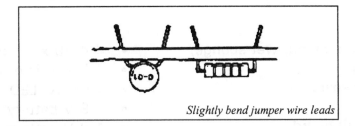

Slightly bend jumper wire leads

4. Solder the jumper wires to the PCB following the "Seven-Step Soldering Procedure."

5. Check for quality: Have a team member assess the quality of the soldered connection. When the team is satisfied that quality standards have been met, have the department supervisor assess for quality.

6. When quality standards have been met, de-solder the jumper wires from the PCB

Training Exercise 4: Soldering and De-Soldering a Simple Circuit on a Printed Circuit Board

In this exercise, trainees practice soldering skills by soldering a simple circuit on a printed circuit board, verify the operation of the circuit, and de-solder the components.

Materials Required:

- Soldering iron, stand, wet sponge, paper towel
- 60/40 alloy solder
- Solder wick
- Printed circuit board
- 4 4-40 nuts
- 4 4-40 x ½" aluminum spacers

- 4 4-40 x ¾" PHMS
- 1 KΩ resistor (BRN-BLK-RED-GLD)
- 1 yellow LED
- 1 9 V battery
- 1 9 V battery clip
- Needle-nose pliers
- Diagonal cutters

1. Insert the 1 KΩ resistor and the yellow LED into the PCB. One lead of the resistor and one lead of the LED must be next to one another on the PC board. (For example, one lead of the resistor in row 15 column O, and one lead of the LED in row 15 column N.)

2. Bend each of the wires on each of the components to hold them during soldering.

3. Solder together the two leads that are next to one another.

4. Connect the 9 V battery clip to the 9 V battery.

5. Touch the black lead of the 9 V battery clip to the resistor and the red lead to the LED.

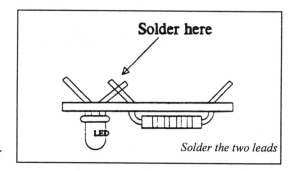
Solder here

Solder the two leads

> Did the LED light? If not, touch the red lead of the 9 V battery clip to the resistor and the black lead to the LED.

> Did the LED light now? If not, ask a team member or the department supervisor for assistance.

6. Check for quality: Have a team member assess the quality of the soldered connection. When the team is satisfied that quality standards have been met, have the department supervisor assess for quality.

7. When quality standards have been met, de-solder the jumper wires from the PCB.

Product #427
For the Week Ending January 8, 19xx

Day	Shift	# Units Assembled	# Units Rejected	Rejection Rate	Accepted Units
Monday	7 am to 3:30 pm	134	29	.216	105
	3 pm to 11:30 pm	120	10		
	11 pm to 7:30 am	90	25		
	Total				
	Average per Shift				
Tuesday	7 am to 3:30 pm	115	35		
	3 pm to 11:30 pm	105	5		
	11 pm to 7:30 am	100	40		
	Total				
	Average per Shift				
Wednesday	7 am to 3:30 pm	125	15		
	3 pm to 11:30 pm	110	0		
	11 pm to 7:30 am	115	20		
	Total				
	Average per Shift				
Thursday	7 am to 3:30 pm	190	75		
	3 pm to 11:30 pm	110	0		
	11 pm to 7:30 am	95	10		
	Total				
	Average per Shift				
Friday	7 am to 3:30 pm	175	55		
	3 pm to 11:30 pm	115	10		
	11 pm to 7:30 am	105	30		
	Total				
	Average per Shift				
Total	7 am to 3:30 pm	739	209		
	3 pm to 11:30 pm	560	25		
	11 pm to 7:30 am	505	125		
	Total	1804	359		
	Average per Shift	601.33	119.67		
Last Week	Total	1710	305		
	Average per Shift	570.0	101.67		
This Week Last Year	Total	1400	70	.05	
	Average per Shift	466.67	23.33		

TekDyne — Employee Time and Production Record

Assembly Department

Employee Name <u>Kelly Masterson</u>

For the Week Ending <u>Friday, January 8, 19xx</u>

Date	Time In	Time Out	Time In	Time Out	Total Hours	Product #	Units Assembled	Units Accepted	Hrs per Accepted Unit
1/4	7:05	11:00	11:30	3:30	7.92	427	6	4	1.98
1/5	7:10	11:00	11:30	3:40	8.0	427	8	5	
1/6	6:55	11:00	11:45	3:30		427	6	4	
1/7	7:00	11:00	11:20	3:30		583	13	13	
1/8	7:00	10:50	11:35	3:30		583	13	12	
Total									

Comments:

Kelly Masterson was assigned to work on Product #427 for three days this week because of another employee's absence. He is normally assigned to the team working on Product #583.

Employee Signature

Kelly Masterson

Supervisor Signature

Pat Belknap

Assembly Department

Product Number: <u>427</u>

Day: <u>Monday, January 4, 19xx</u>   Shift: <u>7:00 a.m. - 3:30 p.m.</u>

Employee	Hours Worked	Total Units Assembled	Hours per Unit	Units Accepted	Hours per Accepted Unit	RATIO Accepted to Rejected
Alioto, M.	8.0	10	.80	9	.89	9:1
Biak, J.	8.08	10		7		
Brown, L.	7.75	9		9		
Chan, W.	8.17	11		11		
Fernandez, A.	7.92	6		5		
Henley, R.	8.0	12		8		
Masterson, K.	7.92	6		4		
Mackie, H.	6.5	8		5		
Ortega, G.	8.0	10		8		
Prentice, P.	8.08	9		5		
Quintara, S.	7.75	11		6		
Stein, M.	7.0	9		8		
Tran, V.	8.0	12		10		
Ventura, S.	7.50	11		10		
Shift Total						

Product #427
For the Week Ending January 8, 19xx

Day	Shift	Employee Hours	Total # Units	# Units Accepted	Hours per Accepted Unit	Decimal Acceptance Rate	Percentage Acceptance Rate
Monday	7 am to 3:30 pm	108.67	134	105	1.035	.78	78%
	3 pm to 11:30 pm		120	110	.962		
	11 pm to 7:30 am	117.33	90	65			
	Total						
	Average per Shift						
Tuesday	7 am to 3:30 pm	143.82	115	80			
	3 pm to 11:30 pm		105	100	.948		
	11 pm to 7:30 am	119.36	100	60			
	Total						
	Average per Shift						
Wednesday	7 am to 3:30 pm		125	110	1.23		
	3 pm to 11:30 pm	96.10	110	110			
	11 pm to 7:30 am		115	95	.991		
	Total						
	Average per Shift						
Thursday	7 am to 3:30 pm	151.92	190	115			
	3 pm to 11:30 pm		110	110	1.042		
	11 pm to 7:30 am	85.935	95	85			
	Total						
	Average per Shift						
Friday	7 am to 3:30 pm		175	120	1.682		
	3 pm to 11:30 pm	118.86	115	105			
	11 pm to 7:30 am		105	75	1.133		
	Total						
	Average per Shift						
Total	7 am to 3:30 pm	741.55	739	530			
	3 pm to 11:30 pm	530.20	560	535			
	11 pm to 7:30 am	501.745	505	380			
	Total		1804	1445	1.227		
	Average per Shift		601.23	481.67			
Last Week	Total	1603.265	1710	1405			
	Average per Shift		570.0	101.67			
This Week Last Year	Total		1400	1330	1.01		
	Average per Shift						

Date: February 20, 19xx
To: TekDyne
From: Marmaduke Systems
Subject: Product #427

TekDyne, please rush information regarding a possible order for Product #427. We need 635 units of this product and would like to know the cost and delivery time before ordering. Please respond with the following information:

Price for 635 units

Delivery time for 635 units

Thanks,
Hank Plato at Marmaduke Systems

From the Desk of Rod McKenzie, Sales and Marketing

Assembly Department—

Before I send a quote on this order, I thought I'd better check with you. I can figure the price, but how long will it take your department to assemble enough units to fill this order?

Please let me know as soon as possible. Also, Ray Nguyn did mention that the price might increase because we have to assemble more parts to make up for defective units. How many units would you have to assemble in order to have 635 accepted units to fill this order?

Thanks,

Rod

TekDyne

MEMORANDUM

Date: March 1, 19xx

To: Trainees, Assembly Department

From: Ted Kutner, CEO

Subject: Critical Thinking

This week you are finishing the assembly of your first TekDyne product, our test warning device. Congratulations on reaching this milestone in your training program. I hope you have enjoyed the training program thus far and that you have developed a sense of the qualities TekDyne seeks and nurtures in its employees. You have no doubt noticed by now that we place a great deal of emphasis on the ability to think critically and to develop creative solutions to problems. This emphasis will continue throughout your training and career with TekDyne.

Swiss psychologist Jean Piaget became well known for his studies in intellectual and cognitive development. His ideas on critical thinking and creative problem solving are expressed in this quote:

> The principal goal of education is to create men (and women) who are capable of doing new things, not simply of repeating what other generations have done—men (and women) who are creative, inventive, and are discoverers.

> The second goal of education is to form minds which can be critical, can verify, and not accept everything that is offered.

At TekDyne we depend on our employees to learn from each other and from experience and to apply knowledge through critical thinking. I encourage each of you to always be alert to finding new ways to do things, to questioning and exploring what you learn, and to recognizing your own innate creativity as one of your most valued personal assets.

Best wishes to you as you progress through the TekDyne training program.

Trainees,

Please use the Problem Solving Model to figure out why we have such a high rejection rate and what we might do to correct it. Copies of the model are attached. Please work with your team to analyze the rejection rate, and let me know whether you found it helpful to organize your thoughts this way.

Problem Solving Model

Adapted from *Keys to Success* by Carol Carter and Sarah Lyman Kravits, Prentice Hall Publishing, 1996

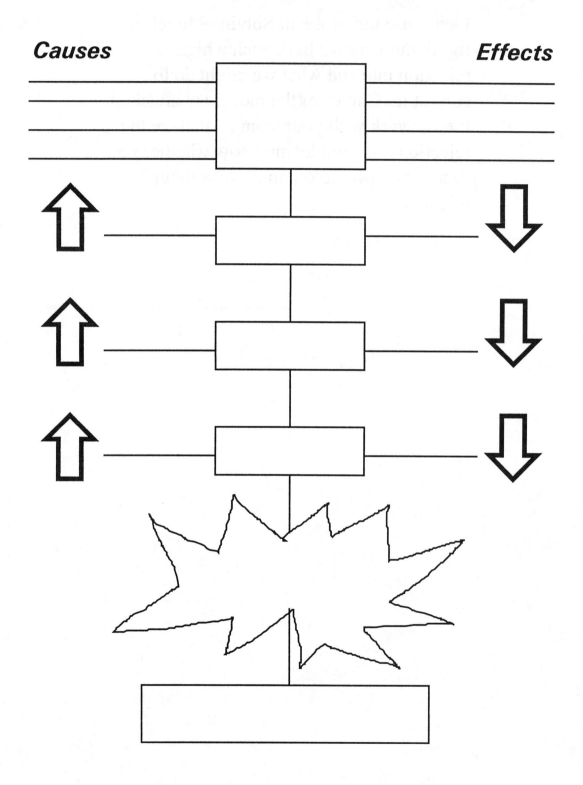

Causes   *Effects*

Problem Solving Model
Adapted from *Keys to Success* by Carol Carter and Sarah Lyman Kravits, Prentice Hall Publishing, 1996

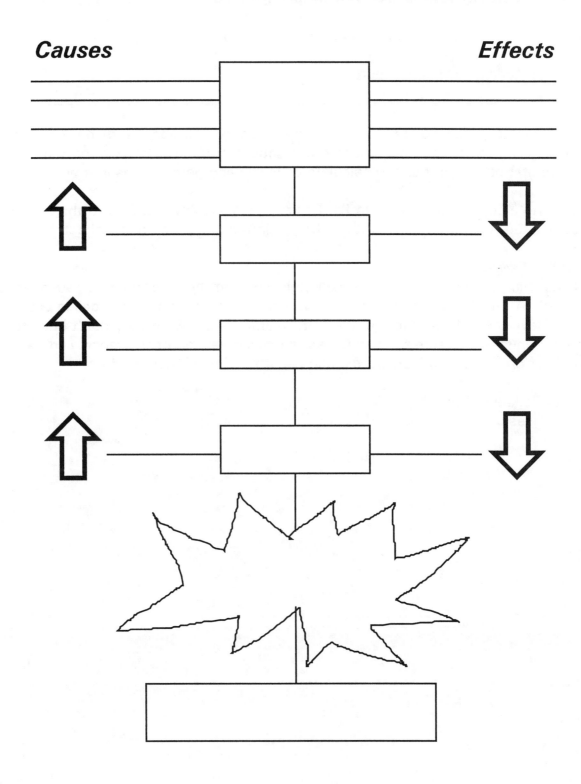

TekDyne

MEMORANDUM

Date: March 2, 19xx

To: Caesar Gutierrez, Parts Department Manager

From: Ray Nguyn, Manufacturing Team Coordinator

Subject: Stock Depletion Report for January

Caesar, I was very disappointed to receive the attached February 18 memo from you. I find it confusing to read a spreadsheet with fractions entered. Did you know that we have computer software that can calculate decimals and percentages in a wink?

I am sending a copy of the report to Pat Belknap in Assembly and also to the trainees who completed this report so that it can be put into a computer spreadsheet.

Note to Pat Belknap:
Pat, If the trainees know how to use Excel, please have them set up a spreadsheet for this report. At least have the trainees convert the fractions to percentages in each column. Have them determine formulas for Columns 7 and 8 so they don't have to calculate manually. Be sure to send Caesar a revised version of the report and save the spreadsheet on the network so Caesar can use it for the February update.

cc: Pat Belknap, Assembly
       Trainees

Attachment

MEMORANDUM

Date: February 18, 19xx

To: Ray Nguyn, Manufacturing Team Coordinator

From: Caesar Gutierrez, Parts Department Manager

Subject: Stock Depletion Report for January

Last month you asked that we keep a record to indicate what fraction of stock is used each week so that we could determine how close our actual depletion is to 1/5 of the inventory each week. The following report provides that information.

Column 1	Column 2	Column 3	Column 4	Column 5	Column 6	Column 7	Column 8
Part Description	Beginning Inventory Level	Fraction Used Week 1	Fraction Used Week 2	Fraction Used Week 3	Fraction Used Week 4	Fraction Remaining	No. Parts Remaining
Scientific Calculator	20	3/20	1/4	1/5	3/10		
Breadboard	35	1/5	8/35	6/35	2/7		
Trimmer Adjustment Tool	200	1/4	1/5	3/10	3/20		
Screw Driver - Philips	30	1/6	1/5	2/15	1/10		
Needle-Nose Pliers	25	4/25	1/5	6/25	3/25		
Diagonal Cutter	35	6/35	1/5	8/35	1/7		
Wire Stripper	25	1/5	4/25	1/5	6/25		
Banana Plug to Minihook - Red	50	4/25	1/5	9/50	6/25		
Banana Plug to Minihook - Black	50	1/25	6/25	1/5	3/25		
Banana Plug to Banana Plug - Red	50	3/25	6/25	1/5	4/25		
Banana Plug to Banana Plug - Black	50	1/5	7/25	2/25	11/50		
10 ft 60/40 Solder	350	12/175	3/25	2/25	11/175		
2 ft Solder Wick	125	26/125	24/125	4/25	23/125		
Soldering Iron Stand	15	1/5	0/0	1/15	4/15		
Soldering Iron - 25 Watt	20	1/4	1/10	1/5	3/20		
Printed Circuit Board	60	1/4	1/5	17/60	1/6		
4-40 Nut	1000	3/20	1/4	1/5	7/40		
4-40 x ½ Aluminum Spacer	350	13/70	71/350	6/35	3/14		
4-40 x ¾ PHMN	200	9/40	1/4	4/25	41/200		
9 Volt Battery Clip	325	12/65	13/65	14/65	56/325		

Date_____   Time_____   Product <u>Test Warning Device/Siren</u>

Employee Name_____   Assembly Date_____

Results: Unit test OK_____   Submit for repair and retest_____

Comments:

_____
_____
_____
_____
_____
_____

Repair Report

Describe problem:_____
_____

Visual inspection results:_____
_____

Test results:_____
_____

Action taken:_____
_____

Parts replaced:_____
_____

Employee Signature:_____   Supervisor Signature:_____

Trainee Self-Evaluation and Transfer Report

Trainee Name	Team Approval	Date	Chapter 3

Performance Record in Assembly Department:

Place a check in the column that best describes your performance in each area:

Area of Training	Outstanding Progress	Shows Improvement	Needs Work
Attitude			
Timeliness of Work			
Attendance/Punctuality			
Accuracy/Thoroughness			
Interest/Team Participation			
Knowledge			
Equipment Proficiency			
Work Habits/Appearance			
Ethics			
Project Points Earned **This Department** Week 1			
Week 2		**Math Proficiency Exam #1**	

Comments:

Department Transferred To: **Repair Department**	Start Date:
Instructor Signature	Trainee Signature

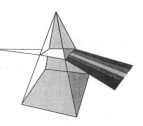

In Basket

Chapter 4
Repair Department

TekDyne Guidelines
Position Description and Training Objectives
Repair Department Trainee

Department Profile

The Repair Department, a branch of Support Services, offers valued services to clients. Products under warranty sometimes fail to operate or require adjustments to maintain precision. When this happens, the Repair Department issues a Return Merchandise Authorization (RMA) to the customer and has the unit returned to TekDyne. Repair Department personnel test the unit, analyze the problem, and repair or replace the product or faulty component. Trainees in this department participate in team troubleshooting activities, maintain repair and quality assurance records, analyze the recorded data, determine standards, and monitor variance from the standards. Trainees continue math and achievement training during their two-week assignment to Repair, with special emphasis on listening and writing as critical elements of effective customer interaction.

Objectives

By the end of the Repair Department module, trainees will:

- Explain and demonstrate the use of scientific and engineering notation.

- Test, troubleshoot, and repair test warning devices.

- Analyze report data as a basis for projections.

- Analyze and identify the essential information provided in a warranty.

- Write a report explaining how one might calculate and use the information provided in the Repair Variance Report

- Identify which information in a repair request is relevant.

- Coach a team on assigned math concepts.

- Locate and price a component at an electronics supply store.

- Write a description of the electronics shopping experience.

- Participate in a team presentation on memory tools and their use.

- Develop a math proficiency exam for the department.

Chapter 4 Projects, Repair Department	
• Repair Variance Report, pp. 95-96 • Repair Variance Analysis, p. 97 • Siren Repair Report, p. 99 • Carlson Electronics, p. 100 • Warranty Comparisons, p. 101 • Test Variance Log, p. 102	• Voice Mail from Rod McKenzie, p. 103 • Dalite Systems, p. 104 • Potentiometer, p. 105 • 529 Power Supply, pp. 106-107 • Voice Mail Messages, pp. 108-109
Math Proficiency, Repair Department	
Exam #2: Powers of Ten	

Module 4-1, Repair Department

Trainee: Your instructor will provide the information necessary to plan your work for the week. Please record this information below for discussion with your team.

Reading Assignments:
    TekDyne Employee Manual, pages_____

_____

_____

Assignments	Due Date	Maximum Points	Special Instructions
TekDyne Employee Manual Assignments			
Additional Assignments			
Total Possible Points This Week:			

Module 4-2, Repair Department

Trainee: *Your instructor will provide the information necessary to plan your work for the week. Please record this information below for discussion with your team.*

Reading Assignments:

TekDyne Employee Manual, pages_____

_____

_____

Assignments	Due Date	Maximum Points	Special Instructions
TekDyne Employee Manual **Assignments**			
Additional Assignments			
Total Possible Points This Week:			

Module 4-1, Repair Department

Team_____   Team Member _____

Performance Expectations: All work is to be thorough, neat, accurate, and completed on time. Teams should assist members in defining outstanding, excellent, satisfactory, and unacceptable performance.

This team member is responsible for completing the following tasks:

Project	Specific Tasks	Special Expectations

Trainee Acceptance of Assignment: I agree to perform the tasks assigned above to the best of my ability and to have my performance on these tasks evaluated constructively by my peers.

Signature: Date:

Team members, please sign below:

_____

_____

_____

Module 4-2, Repair Department

Team_____   Team Member _____

Performance Expectations: All work is to be thorough, neat, accurate, and completed on time. Teams should assist members in defining outstanding, excellent, satisfactory, and unacceptable performance.

This team member is responsible for completing the following tasks:

Project	Specific Tasks	Special Expectations

Trainee Acceptance of Assignment: I agree to perform the tasks assigned above to the best of my ability and to have my performance on these tasks evaluated constructively by my peers.

Signature: Date:

Team members, please sign below:

_____

_____

_____

Employee Development Program Team Performance Evaluation

Module 4-1, Repair Department

Team _____

Team Worker of the Week
This team member is recognized for outstanding team support and earns a 5% grade bonus.

As a team, evaluate each member on task performance and on group interaction by checking one line in each column. Be certain that the team agrees on the meanings of each level of performance.

Team Member:	Name		Name		Name		Name	
	Task	Group	Task	Group	Task	Group	Task	Group
Outstanding								
Excellent								
Satisfactory								
Needs Improvement								
Limited Progress								

Grade Distribution
This team agrees that members contributed the following percentages of work this week and will earn the following percentage of the portfolio grade (percentages must total 100%).

Percentage:				
Grade: *To be completed by instructor*				

Self-Assessment
Use one word to describe your overall rating of your own performance this week. Explain any difference between the team evaluation and your self-assessment in the Comments section below.

My Performance:				
Comment on your attitude, timeliness of work, attendance, punctuality, accuracy, thoroughness, interest, knowledge, equipment proficiency, work habits, appearance, ethics.				
Team Member Signatures:				

Employee Development Program   Team Performance Evaluation

Module 4-2, Repair Department

Team _____

Team Worker of the Week
This team member is recognized for outstanding team support and earns a 5% grade bonus.

As a team, evaluate each member on task performance and on group interaction by checking one line in each column. Be certain that the team agrees on the meanings of each level of performance.

Team Member:	Name		Name		Name		Name	
	Task	Group	Task	Group	Task	Group	Task	Group
Outstanding								
Excellent								
Satisfactory								
Needs Improvement								
Limited Progress								

Grade Distribution
This team agrees that members contributed the following percentages of work this week and will earn the following percentage of the portfolio grade (percentages must total 100%).

Percentage:				
Grade: To be completed by instructor				

Self-Assessment
Use one word to describe your overall rating of your own performance this week. Explain any difference between the team evaluation and your self-assessment in the Comments section below.

My Performance:				
Comment on your attitude, timeliness of work, attendance, punctuality, accuracy, thoroughness, interest, knowledge, equipment proficiency, work habits, appearance, ethics.				
Team Member Signatures:				

TekDyne Guidelines
Variance Calculation

Definitions:
- *Variance*: A difference between what is expected and what actually occurs.
- *Standard*: A point of reference which allows quantitative measurement.

TekDyne has established procedures to ensure that units shipped to customers are of the highest quality. Defective or incorrect components, faulty assembly, weak soldering connections, exposure to elements, and accidental breakage sometimes cause a small percentage of shipped units to become inoperable during the warranty period. Through careful monitoring and analysis of RMA records, TekDyne estimates that the number of such units returned for repair each month is approximately 1 percent of the units shipped in a month.

$$\text{Standard} = (1\%) \times (\text{number shipped})$$

The actual number of units returned for repair may be more or less than the standard 1 percent. The number over or under the standard is the variance.

$$\text{Variance} = (\text{number returned}) - (\text{standard})$$

Example: In April 1425 units were shipped and 11 units were returned for repair.

$$\text{Standard} = (1\%) \times (1425) = 14.25$$
$$\text{Variance} = 11 - 14.25 = -3.25$$

The **negative** number (−3.25) tells us that there were fewer units returned than expected. When the variance for any month is a **positive** number, it means more repairs than expected. When this happens, the Repair Department must attempt to find the reason for the increased number of repairs.

Product #368

12-Months Ending February 19xx

Month	# Units Shipped	RMA Standard[1]	RMA Actual	Variance[2]
March	1425	14.25	11	−3.25
April	1267		8	
May	1411		12	
June	1232		6	
July	1358		15	
August	1692		17	
September	1231		22	
October	1287		21	
November	1014		22	
December	1196		6	
January	1352		6	
February	1406		5	
12-Month Total				
12-Month Average				
12-Month Range[3]				

[1]Standard is set at 1% of the number of units produced for the month.
[2]Use negative numbers to indicate variance *under* the RMA standard; positive to indicate *over*.
[3]Difference between the 12-month high and the 12-month low.

TekDyne

MEMORANDUM

Date: March 10, 19xx

To: Robert Monroe, Repair Department Manager

From: Cecil Tandy, Support Services Team Coordinator

Subject: Repair Variance Analysis

Robert, the new report you have developed for monitoring repair variance looks as though it could be very useful, but I am not sure I understand it well enough to be able to present it at the Executive Team Meeting next week.

Would you please have your department prepare a written explanation of the report for me by next week. It will be helpful if they explain what the numbers mean and how they are calculated. Can this report be used to identify trends? How can it assist the Executive Team in planning? Does it provide any help in forecasting personnel or inventory needs? What information does it give me about the past twelve months that could be helpful in projecting the next twelve months? Could any of this information be useful in determining unit selling prices?

I would like this information to be in the form of a written report that I can attach to the Repair Variance Report when I distribute it at the meeting.

Thanks for your help.

Troubleshooting Guide

Troubleshooting requires that you take a clear and objective look at the product to determine the symptoms. That done, you can begin looking for the possible causes. TekDyne maintains a separate diagnostic chart for each product. (See European Siren Instruction Booklet.) In most cases, this information will be sufficient to determine the problem and solve it.

Checklist

⇨ Did you follow the testing instructions accurately?

⇨ Do the soldering connections meet TekDyne soldering standards? (Review Soldering Procedures, Chapter 3.)

⇨ Are there any soldering bridges to interfere with correct operation?

⇨ Were the correct components installed?

⇨ Were the components correctly installed at the right locations?

⇨ Are there any loose wires, solder, or other foreign matter interfering with operation?

⇨ After you checked the above, did a team member also check?

If the answers above are positive, refer to the product assembly instructions, troubleshooting section, for additional diagnostics and solutions information.

TekDyne

Quality Inspection Report

Date_____ Time_____ Product <u>Test Warning Device/Siren</u>

Employee Name_____ Assembly Date_____

Results: Unit test OK_____ Submit for repair and retest_____

Comments:

_____
_____
_____
_____
_____
_____

Repair Report

Describe problem:_____
_____

Visual inspection results:_____
_____

Test results:_____
_____

Action taken:_____
_____

Parts replaced:_____
_____

Employee Signature:_____ Supervisor Signature:_____

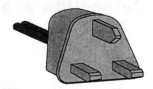

Carlson Electronics

**1965 Circuit Boulevard
Brentwood, NJ 10034**

March 12, 19xx

Mr. Robert Monroe
Repair Department Manager
TekDyne
One TekDyne Circle
Livermore, CA 94123

Dear Bob:

It's been a long time since I last saw you, and I hope things are going well with you. We have been so busy I haven't had time to keep up with old friends in the business.

Actually, the reason I'm writing today is that I am having a problem with the new 529 Power Supply. We bought it in January, and it worked just great until last week. I can't figure out what's wrong with it. Sometimes it works fine, sometimes it seems really haywire, and sometimes it just plain won't work! I've never seen anything quite like it!

I remember that when we used to buy our power supplies from Mike Jones we ran into problems all the time, but this is unusual for equipment from TekDyne. We have always been so pleased with your power supplies that we wouldn't think of ordering from any other manufacturer.

I know we can count on you to repair or replace the power supply, so I am writing to ask for an RMA number. As soon as you can get that to me, I will ship the power supply back. Of course, having to be without the power supply while you fix it is going to be a hardship, so I am hoping you will just replace it with a new one immediately so that we won't be without equipment any longer than necessary.

I look forward to hearing from you. Next time you're in New Jersey, let's get together! Margie often asks about you, and you haven't met our newest family member yet.

Sincerely,

Hank

Hank Carlson
President

> *Repair Department, please check
> on Hank's warranty and draft a
> response. I would like your
> recommendation as to how we
> should handle this.*
>
> *Robert*

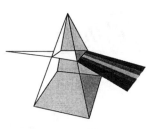

TekDyne
Creating Tomorrow's Solutions Today

One TekDyne Circle, Livermore, CA 94123

Five-Year Limited Warranty
Power Supply
TekDyne Product 529

Within five (5) years from date of purchase you may return your TekDyne 529 Power Supply for repair or adjustment for a service charge of $25.

After five (5) years from date of purchase you may return your TekDyne 529 Power Supply for repair or adjustment for labor charges of $55 per hour plus parts and postage, payable in advance.

All returned merchandise must be accompanied by a TekDyne return merchandise authorization (RMA).

Products that have been modified in any way, or that show evidence of misuse, neglect, or accident, will be repaired and returned at the owner's expense. Prior to making such repairs, TekDyne will require written authorization for billing repair charges.

TekDyne reserves the right to either repair or replace a product covered by this warranty.

When returning a product, enclose a copy of the RMA and a check for $25. Ship the product postage paid and insured to:

Repair Department
TekDyne
One TekDyne Circle
Livermore, CA 94123

> *Trainees, would you please locate some other types of warranties for comparison. Determine what information must be included and whether we are missing anything. Thanks, Robert.*

Test Meter Readings, Product #529

RMA Units, March 19xx

Customer	Date	Before Repair	After Repair	Correction	Tech
Abernathy Equipment	3/22/xx	-32.11	120.00	+152.11	EM
Bestech Industries	3/2/xx	0	122.14		PC
Deltaflow	3/11/xx	-123.42	121.76		SS
Franklin Smith Co.	3/6/xx	136.21	121.55		LS
Ho Electronics	3/30/xx	6.14	120.68		EM
Jamail Technotics	3/15/xx	-71.22	120.02		LS
Kinto Keys	3/21/xx	-14.33	122.03		CO
LML Equipment	3/5/xx	32.89	121.14		CO
Monroe Specialties	3/12/xx	-0.24	122.84		LS
Muzik Majik	3/28/xx	173.65	121.35		PC
Oregon Electronics	3/19/xx	42.32	121.95		LS
Pantheon Supplies	3/6/xx	-86.27	120.89		EM
PyroTechnix	3/4/xx	-192.75	122.18		PC
Roseville Equipment	3/25/xx	-23.56	120.73		SS
Average					
Variance*					

*Variance is the total difference between the lowest reading and the highest reading for each column.

Voice Mail Message Transcription

Hi Bob, it's Rod McKenzie in Sales and Marketing. I've got a little problem I hope you can help me with. I recently got a new laptop to use on my sales trips, and it's really helpful—as long as I'm in the US, that is!

There seems to be a difference in the type of wiring used in Europe, and I can't use my laptop when I'm there. I was wondering if there is some way you can adapt my laptop so that I can use it in London and Paris as well as in Seattle and Cincinnati. (My wife suggested a VERRRRY long extension cord, but she doesn't know very much about electronics!)

Would you please give me a call and let me know what you suggest. I appreciate your help.

DALITE SYSTEMS
25 WEST 39TH STREET
SERENDIPITY, WY 67143

March 13, 19xx

Trainees,
I don't have time to try to understand
what Dalite is asking. Would you
please underline the important
information and make a recommendation
for handling this.
Thanks,
Robert

TekDyne
One TekDyne Circle
Livermore, CA 94123

Dear Sir:

The TekDyne Power Supply, Product Number 529, which we bought on January 14, Purchase Order Number 46837 signed by Raoul Seguin, does not work properly. The Power Supply was delivered on January 21 by A-Best Trucking Company. The delivery person, Micky, was very careful with the Power Supply, and everyone who uses it here has been properly trained to do so.

I don't know what the problem is. At 3:14 p.m. last Monday our technician, Randall White, reported that the power supply was working erratically. Randall was working on a rush job for a very important client when this happened, and he was quite upset. Then at 5:29 p.m. Randall reported that the power supply was okay. By the time our night technician, Marcia Pendleton, came on duty the power supply was not working at all.

The next day Randall reported that the power supply was again not working properly. In one case the reading was off by a lot, and in another it was only slightly off. I cannot figure out what is wrong with this thing. Our bookkeeper, Joyce Madison, thinks the problem is due to the cold spell we have been having. Maybe she is right. You should check that. Randall and Marcia think it has something to do with the resistors you used. I don't know what the problem is, but I do know we can't use the power supply the way it is. We can't depend on it at all.

If you need more information, you can call me at 602-496-8080. I will be on vacation for a couple days, but otherwise I'm usually in the office. I do sometimes take a long lunch, but you can probably reach me later on those days.

Yours truly,

George Snow

George Snow
Senior Technician

E-MAIL FOR REPAIRS

Date:	March 12, 19xx
To:	Repair Department
From:	Parts Department
Subject:	10KΩ +/-20%, ¾ Watt Potentiometer

We are unable to supply the 10KΩ +/-20%, ¾ Watt Potentiometers you requested for Product 529 repairs. You have requisitioned an unexpectedly high number of these components this month and have depleted the stock. We have placed an additional order for the component, but it will be several weeks before they can be delivered.

I understand that you still need more of these components because of a problem that seems to be common to many of the 529s shipped in January. I would suggest that you send the technicians to an electronics supply store to purchase an emergency supply of the components.

Let me know if it looks like you will need an increased supply of these components for next month so that we can plan ahead. Also, let me know if it appears that the original components were faulty. We rarely use so many of these components, and I am becoming concerned that we may have purchased a batch of defective components from Grayline. If so, we will have to find a new supplier. Let me know where you find the parts and how much they are selling for.

Return-Merchandise Authorizations
March, 19xx

Customer	Product Number	Purchase Date	Problem	RMA #	Tech
Bestech	529	1/xx	Functions erratically, sometimes not at all	52931	TS
PyroTech	529	1/xx	Unreliable, sometimes inoperable	52932	VV
Roseville	368	10/xx	Needs calibration	36833	DC
LML	529	1/xx	Only works sometimes	52934	SS
Pantheon	529	1/xx	Not always reliable	52935	EM
Franklin	529	1/xx	Unreliable	52936	DS
Deltaflow	529	1/xx	Functions erratically	52937	TS
Bestech	418	7/xx	Adjust meters	41838	DC
Monroe	529	1/xx	Operating strangely; not reliable	52939	VV
Jamail	529	1/xx	Sometimes doesn't work	52940	SS
Oregon	529	1/xx	Erratic operation	52941	DC
Abernathy	529	1/xx	Not working properly sometimes	52942	TS
Kinto	529	1/xx	Inaccurate; sometimes won't work at all	52943	DS
Muzik	529	1/xx	Fails to work properly sometimes	52944	SS
Ho	529	1/xx	Unreliable performance	52945	VV
Justice	272	10/xx	Replace cracked lense	27246	DS
Carlson	529	1/xx	Erratic operation	52947	TS
Dalite	529	1/xx	Erratic operation	52948	TS

E-MAIL FOR REPAIRS

Date: March 15, 19xx
To: Repair Department
From: Robert Monroe
Subject: 529 Power Supply

This month's RMA log shows repairs requested for an incredibly high number of 529 Power Supplies. Would you please get together and figure out what is going on here. Mr. Kutner will want to know how this problem developed, and you are the best people to ask. Please prepare a team report with any information you can come up with about these power supplies so that we might track the problem and solve it. I think a brainstorming session would be a good first step.

TekDyne

MEMORANDUM

Date: March 20, 19xx

To: Support Services Team Employees

From: Cecil Tandy, Support Services Team Coordinator

Subject: Listening to Customers

Last week I attended a seminar on customer service and was surprised to find that the major topic covered was LISTENING! The seminar facilitator repeatedly emphasized the importance of this skill in interacting with customers, and I learned a great deal about how we can better serve our customers by listening to what they have to say.

The following steps are very helpful. Read them, learn them, and use them every day. I know you will make our customers happy, and I'll bet even your friends and family will be favorably impressed.

- Stop what you are doing and listen with your whole body and mind. Too frequently customers become frustrated when employees seem preoccupied or too busy to talk to them.

- Take a learning approach to listening and hear the customer out before you begin to develop a response. Try to understand the customer's position before trying to get the customer to understand yours.

- Don't make judgments about the customer or his position. Your openness will enable you to hear the problem without taking a defensive attitude.

- Pay close attention so that you don't miss any details. Use your power of concentration to keep from drifting if the conversation becomes boring or repetitive.

- Check your understanding by paraphrasing what the customer has said. You can eliminate a lot of misunderstandings this way.

Because this skill is so important, I would like all of you to participate in some listening exercises in the department. Take turns reading the following voice mail messages to each other, take notes, and check to see how well you listened. The listening partner may not look at the messages while they are being read.

Voice Mail Message Transcription

The following voice mail message was recorded at 6:58 a.m. on March 20:

Hello! This is Paula Heinz with Janna Ray Supplies in St. Helen, Arkansas, 315-496-2000. We're having a terrible time with our new power supply, model 529. We just bought it in January, and it is doing the strangest things. One day it works fine and the next day it doesn't work at all. I would like an RMA number so that I can send the power supply back to you for repairs. Please call me at your earliest convenience.

The following voice mail message was recorded at 7:12 a.m. on March 20:

Hi. My name is Lester Philpott and I am a customer service representative with TruTech Distributors. We are having a serious problem with the 529 power supply we bought from you last January. It really is amazing that in only two months a product for which we paid a lot of money could be having problems. Whether you know it or not, when your equipment fails TruTech is unable to take care of our customers and we get pretty unhappy about that. I don't know what you plan to do to correct this problem, but you had better do it fast. Call me back at 325-9857 and let me know how you plan to handle this problem. If I don't hear from you tomorrow I will take other steps to settle this matter. After all, there are other manufacturers of power supplies, and their power supplies probably work a lot better than yours.

The following voice mail message was recorded at 7:31 a.m. on March 20:

This is Jean Nelson at Arbor Electronics in Dallas. We need some help. Our building was damaged in a storm last week and part of the ceiling fell in on some of our equipment. The old 142 power supply we bought from you 9 years ago was damaged. The outer case has a crack in it and it is not working at all. How can I find out if it is still covered by warranty? If it is not covered by warranty can you still repair it? Would it make more sense to buy a new one? Please call me at 601-492-5800 as soon as you can. Thanks.

Trainee Self-Evaluation and Transfer Report

Trainee Name	Team Approval	Date	Chapter
			4

Performance Record in Repair Department:

Place a check in the column that best describes your performance in each area:

Area of Training	Outstanding Progress	Shows Improvement	Needs Work
Attitude			
Timeliness of Work			
Attendance/Punctuality			
Accuracy/Thoroughness			
Interest/Team Participation			
Knowledge			
Equipment Proficiency			
Work Habits/Appearance			
Ethics			

Project Points Earned This Department Week 1			
Week 2		Math Proficiency Exam #2	

Comments:

Department Transferred To:	Start Date:
Help Desk	
Instructor Signature	Trainee Signature

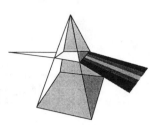

In Basket

Chapter 5
Help Desk

TekDyne Guidelines

Position Description and Training Objectives
Help Desk Trainee

Department Profile

Help Desk employees provide a broad array of services to customers and to other TekDyne departments. They give prompt and courteous answers to questions about TekDyne products and they also assist employees with helpful tips and guidance on computer topics. The Help Desk has become such a highly respected team at TekDyne that members are frequently consulted on topics outside their assigned areas. Trainees assigned to this department respond to Help Desk requests for information and guidance, log questions and problems as they are received, participate in team problem-solving, and follow up to determine that problems have been resolved. While assigned to the Help Desk, trainees continue to participate in math and achievement training with emphasis on stress management through mental and physical health.

Objectives

By the end of the Help Desk module, trainees will:

- Convert metric units to US customary units and US customary units to metric units.

- Explain the use of metrics in area, weight, volume, and temperature.

- Define electrical current prefixes.

- Participate in a team presentation on health issues and describe methods to maintain physical and mental health.

- Explain the dangers of substance abuse and sexual harassment in the workplace.

- Participate in team brainstorming sessions to solve problems.

- Analyze and investigate an incident report and develop a recommendation.

- Use error codes to troubleshoot a hardware problem.

- Explain the value of motivation, commitment, responsibility, and initiative as personal power boosters.

- Identify resources available for basic electronics information.

Chapter 5 Projects, Help Desk	
• Fitness Guidelines, p. 121	• Voice Mail, Overite Industries, p. 130
• Number Conversions, p. 122	• Electrical Current Prefixes, p. 131
• Metric Conversions, pp. 124-125	• Voice Mail, Buck Boston, p. 132
• RMA #52963, p. 126	• Peer Investigative Panel, pp. 133-134
• Peg Nixon's Dilemma, p. 127	• Diem Nhu E-Mail, p. 135-136
• Unit Prefixes, p. 128	• Help Desk Log, pp. 137-138
• Trouble with Vern, p. 129	• Information Resources, p. 139
Math Proficiency, Help Desk	
Exam #3: Units and Prefixes	

Module 5-1, Help Desk

Trainee: *Your instructor will provide the information necessary to plan your work for the week. Please record this information below for discussion with your team.*

Reading Assignments:
   TekDyne Employee Manual, pages_____
   _____
   _____

Assignments	Due Date	Maximum Points	Special Instructions
TekDyne Employee Manual Assignments			
Additional Assignments			
Total Possible Points This Week:			

Module 5-2, Help Desk

Trainee: *Your instructor will provide the information necessary to plan your work for the week. Please record this information below for discussion with your team.*

Reading Assignments:

TekDyne Employee Manual, pages_____

_____

_____

Assignments	Due Date	Maximum Points	Special Instructions
TekDyne Employee Manual Assignments			
Additional Assignments			
Total Possible Points This Week:			

Module 5-1, Help Desk

Team_____   Team Member _____

Performance Expectations: All work is to be thorough, neat, accurate, and completed on time. Teams should assist members in defining outstanding, excellent, satisfactory, and unacceptable performance.

This team member is responsible for completing the following tasks:

Project	Specific Tasks	Special Expectations

Trainee Acceptance of Assignment: I agree to perform the tasks assigned above to the best of my ability and to have my performance on these tasks evaluated constructively by my peers.

Signature: Date:

Team members, please sign below:

_____

_____

_____

Module 5-2, Help Desk

Team_____   Team Member _____

Performance Expectations: All work is to be thorough, neat, accurate, and completed on time. Teams should assist members in defining outstanding, excellent, satisfactory, and unacceptable performance.

This team member is responsible for completing the following tasks:

Project	Specific Tasks	Special Expectations

Trainee Acceptance of Assignment: I agree to perform the tasks assigned above to the best of my ability and to have my performance on these tasks evaluated constructively by my peers.

Signature: Date:

Team members, please sign below:

_____

_____

_____

Module 5-1, Help Desk

Team _____

Team Worker of the Week
This team member is recognized for outstanding team support and earns a 5% grade bonus.

As a team, evaluate each member on task performance and on group interaction by checking one line in each column. Be certain that the team agrees on the meanings of each level of performance.

Team Member:	Name		Name		Name		Name	
	Task	Group	Task	Group	Task	Group	Task	Group
Outstanding								
Excellent								
Satisfactory								
Needs Improvement								
Limited Progress								

Grade Distribution
This team agrees that members contributed the following percentages of work this week and will earn the following percentage of the portfolio grade (percentages must total 100%).

Percentage:				
Grade: To be completed by instructor				

Self-Assessment
Use one word to describe your overall rating of your own performance this week. Explain any difference between the team evaluation and your self-assessment in the Comments section below.

My Performance:				
Comment on your attitude, timeliness of work, attendance, punctuality, accuracy, thoroughness, interest, knowledge, equipment proficiency, work habits, appearance, ethics.				
Team Member Signatures:				

Module 5-2, Help Desk

Team _____

Team Worker of the Week
This team member is recognized for outstanding team support and earns a 5% grade bonus.

As a team, evaluate each member on task performance and on group interaction by checking one line in each column. Be certain that the team agrees on the meanings of each level of performance.

Team Member:	Name		Name		Name		Name	
	Task	Group	Task	Group	Task	Group	Task	Group
Outstanding								
Excellent								
Satisfactory								
Needs Improvement								
Limited Progress								

Grade Distribution
This team agrees that members contributed the following percentages of work this week and will earn the following percentage of the portfolio grade (percentages must total 100%).

Percentage:				
Grade: To be completed by instructor				

Self-Assessment
Use one word to describe your overall rating of your own performance this week. Explain any difference between the team evaluation and your self-assessment in the Comments section below.

My Performance:				
Comment on your attitude, timeliness of work, attendance, punctuality, accuracy, thoroughness, interest, knowledge, equipment proficiency, work habits, appearance, ethics.				
Team Member Signatures:				

TekDyne
MEMORANDUM

Date: March 18, 19xx

To: Tim Hernandez, Help Desk Manager

From: Christine Bennett, Human Resources Manager

Subject: Fitness Guidelines

Tim, I know this is an unusual request for the Help Desk, but you are certainly accustomed to unusual requests! I am working on a special project and am writing to request the help of your department.

I want to prepare a brochure outlining fitness guidelines for our employees. I think it will be helpful for them to understand the important roles physical and mental health play in their lives. We hear so much about stress today, and I recently read an outstanding book that had some tips for reducing stress. Did you know that by eating the right foods (and in the right quantities!) and getting sufficient exercise and sleep we can reduce our stress levels and avoid the depression that often accompanies stress?

The people who work at the Help Desk have helpful, cheery attitudes all the time; yet they work in a hectic environment where they respond to calls from internal and external clients. When people call in with problems, they are sometimes frustrated and irate. I know your department has developed techniques for not allowing the problems of others to dampen their spirits. I would like them to share some of their secrets with the rest of the company.

Please have your teams create brochures on the following topics:

Nutrition, Exercise, Sleep, Stress Management, Depression

There is some excellent information available on the Internet, and I have seen a lot of magazine articles on these subjects. A two-page brochure would work nicely, but be sure the writers include some graphics and different fonts to give it a professional appearance. I will need the brochures by next Monday.

I really do appreciate your taking this on, and I look forward to seeing the final products next week.

E·MAIL FOR HELP DESK

Date:	March 18, 19xx
To:	Help Desk
From:	Pam Chavez, Sales and Marketing
Subject:	Number Conversions

I just received an order for replacement parts from a company in Brazil, and for some reason they specified the parts in scientific notation. Would you please convert each item to the correct metric prefix so that I can proceed to fill the order?

Thanks for your help!

Pam

Quantity	Scientific Notation Value	Metric Prefix
10	$6.8 \times 10^3 \Omega$	$6.8\ K\Omega$
10	$910 \times 10^3 \Omega$	
25	$1 \times 10^7 \Omega$	
5	$1 \times 10^{-4} f$	
15	$4.7 \times 10^{-2} f$	
50	$4.7 \times 10^{-5} f$	
50	$1 \times 10^{-9} f$	
25	$2.7 \times 10^{-1} f$	
10	$2.2 \times 10^{-6} H$	
30	$5.6 \times 10^{-8} H$	
5	$6.8 \times 10^{-7} H$	

Sample Flow Chart

Help Desk Procedure

The Help Desk provides technical support to all departments in the organization. When employees or customers experience problems with equipment or are uncertain about how to use a computer software function, they may call the Help Desk number for assistance. The Help Desk operator will either resolve the problem over the telephone or arrange for a technician to visit the site.

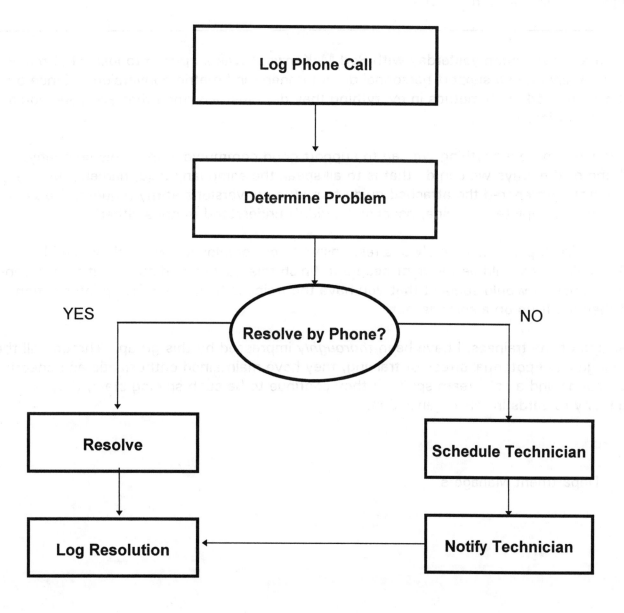

TekDyne

MEMORANDUM

Date: March 24, 19xx

To: Tim Hernandez, Help Desk Manager

From: Ted Kutner, CEO

Subject: Metric Conversions

Tim, in a conversation yesterday with Rod McKenzie, I was surprised to learn that many of our administrative support personnel do not understand metric conversions. Since our technicians work with metrics in everything they do, I just assumed that everyone could convert metrics.

I would like to do everything we can to support good communication in this company, and one of the ways we can do that is to all speak the same language; namely, metrics. My secretary prepared the attached guide to metric conversions at my request. He was not able to complete the guide, because he didn't understand metrics either!

The Help Desk personnel are always responsive to our employees when they need help, and I think they would be the right people to finish this guide and distribute it to everyone for reference. I would suggest that you have the trainees fill in the missing information and then set it up on a spreadsheet.

Speaking of the trainees, I have been *thoroughly* impressed by this group. Through all the challenges and potential stress of training, they have maintained enthusiastic and cheerful dispositions and a solid team spirit. If they continue to be such shining stars, they will find many rewards in this organization.

Thanks.

cc: Department Managers

Metric Conversion Guide

U.S. Customary			Metric	
1 inch	=	2.54		centimeters
1 foot	=			centimeters
1 yard	=			meters
1 mile	=			kilometers
1 sq. inch	=			sq. centimeters
1 sq. foot	=			sq. meters
1 sq. yard	=			sq. meters
1 sq. mile	=			sq. kilometers
1 acre	=			hectares
1 ounce	=			grams
1 pound	=			kilograms
1 short ton	=			tonnes
1 teaspoon	=			milliliters
1 tablespoon	=			milliliters
1 fluid ounce	=			milliliters
1 cup	=			liters
1 pint	=			liters
1 quart	=			liters
1 gallon	=			liters
1 cubic foot	=			cubic meters
1 cubic yard	=			cubic meters
1 degree Fahrenheit	=			degrees Celsius

E·MAIL FOR HELP DESK

Date: March 22, 19xx
To: Help Desk
From: ElekTek Systems
Subject: RMA #52963

I spoke with Robert Monroe in your Repair Department yesterday and he gave me an RMA to return some equipment for repairs. My problem is that I can't figure out how to ship it.

The owner's manual says the equipment weighs 23 kilograms. It also specifies that when shipping it should be placed in a 38 cm x 32 cm x 28 cm carton with padding. Please translate this to U.S. pounds and inches and email this information to me so that I can send the equipment back today.

Thank you,

Chris Flagstaff

Peg Nixon's Dilemma

During lunch today you shared a table with Peg Nixon from the Assembly Department. Peg has been with TekDyne for a very long time, and you became good friends when you were training in Assembly. Today's conversation, however, has left you feeling troubled.

Peg told you she was worried about one of her coworkers, whose name she did not want to reveal, and she insisted that you promise not to repeat her story to anyone.

Peg proceeded to tell you that she has worked with this friend (we'll call him Buddy) for the past nine years. During all that time she had enormous respect for him. He was reliable, considerate, competent, and pleasant. He never took advantage of his team members, and he always did his share of the work.

Peg said that Buddy has changed dramatically over the last few weeks, and that she is alarmed and concerned about his behavior. Buddy has started coming to work late, and Peg said she has been clocking him in so that he won't get in trouble. Now she feels guilty and is worried that *she* will be the one to get in trouble.

Buddy has also been making a lot of mistakes in assembling units, and several times Peg found him asleep in his car when he should have been on the job. When she tries to talk to Buddy about her concerns, he becomes irritable and tells her to mind her own business. Peg is afraid that Buddy's behavior is hurting the team, the department, the company, and himself. She said that yesterday he fell asleep at his workstation and burned himself on his soldering iron. Peg suspects that Buddy is drinking at work because she sometimes smells alcohol on his breath.

Peg says she wants to continue to protect Buddy, because she knows he needs his job. She reported hearing a rumor that Buddy's son is terminally ill and that Buddy and his wife are separating. Peg doesn't want to do anything that would add to Buddy's problems, but she feels she must do something to help him.

The lunch break ended before you could advise Peg, but she said she would stop by the Help Desk tomorrow to see if you have any suggestions.

What will you say to Peg?

TekDyne
MEMORANDUM

Date: March 24, 19xx

To: Tim Hernandez, Help Desk Manager

From: Christine Bennett, Human Resources

Subject: Unit Prefixes

Tim, in working with the trainees, will you please emphasize the importance of learning unit prefixes. As you know, technicians use unit prefixes everyday in their work. It is imperative that trainees learn them now while they are still in training. To reinforce their knowledge, please have them complete the following exercise:

Which prefix is most appropriately used to measure the following distances in feet?

Distance from Earth to the Sun (92.9 million miles)   _____

Distance from Earth to the Moon (384,400 km)   _____

Average depth of the Pacific Ocean (4282 m)   _____

Distance from New York City to Orlando, Florida (1100 miles) _____

Diameter of a wood screw   _____

Height of the world's tallest building
(Petronas Towers in Kuala Lumpur, Malaysia, 452 meters)   _____

Length of an ant's antenna   _____

MEMORANDUM

Date: March 27, 19xx

To: Tim Hernandez, Help Desk Manager

From: Ted Kutner, CEO

Subject: Electrical Current Prefixes, Abbreviations, and Values

---

Tim, I dropped by your department yesterday to see how things were going, but you were gone to the conflict-resolution seminar in San Francisco. I hope it was a good seminar and that you brought back lots of useful information.

While I was in your area, I took the time to chat with some of your staff. What a great crew you have assembled! I just don't know how they can handle so many different types of calls so efficiently. Vern made a suggestion yesterday which I want to implement right away. We had been talking about the Metric Conversion Guide you put together for the rest of the company, and Vern said that it would be great to have a chart identifying current prefixes, abbreviations, and values.

Would you please have your department create a poster showing this information. I would like to have copies made to post in each department, so have them make it as professional and attractive as possible. After all, if the employees will refer to their chart instead of calling Help, it will reduce the amount of work your department has to do!

Voice Mail Message Transcription

Help Desk—it's Buck Boston from Field Services. I'm calling from the cell phone in my truck because I have the most unbelievable emergency and I don't know what to do. PLEASE call me back as soon as you can.

I was driving along enjoying the view and drove into a tunnel with a low overhead. I didn't get very far before the truck got stuck. Now it's wedged under the tunnel ceiling, and I can't get it to move forward or backward. You are good at solving problems. Tell me what to do to get out of this jam! I'm waiting for your call at 321-9087.

TekDyne
MEMORANDUM

Date: March 28, 19xx

To: Help Desk Trainee

From: Christine Bennett, Human Resources

Subject: Peer Investigative Panel Assignment

The TekDyne disciplinary process allows for any employee to request a Peer Investigative Panel recommendation prior to disciplinary action. The purpose of this panel is to investigate the circumstances of the described incident and to develop a recommendation for action. Employees are assigned to the panel through a process of random selection. Your name has been selected to serve on this committee in an incident involving employee Margaret Montague.

The situation to be investigated by the panel is described in the attached incident report. Please be thorough and fair in your investigation and assessment of the situation. Your recommendation should fall within legal requirements and should be based on factual information.

While the Peer Investigative Panel functions in an advisory capacity, it is an extremely effective way for the organization and its employees to share differing perspectives. Your participation in this investigation is sincerely appreciated. Please forward your panel's recommendation to me within one week so that I can review your recommendation prior to taking action.

TekDyne Employee Disciplinary Process

1st Offense   Oral reprimand
2nd Offense   Written reprimand
3rd Offense   Termination

Any offense involving violation of law, violation of safety procedures,
or threat of violence may result in immediate termination.

Attachment

Statement of Incident

In an annual update of software site licensing agreements it was learned that TekDyne has no license for the SOUNDS AND LIGHT presentation software currently available on the network. A preliminary investigation indicated that employee Margaret Montague copied this software from a former employer and installed it on the TekDyne network without benefit of a license and without approval by her supervisor.

Reported by: Tully Panabos, Admin. Svcs. Team Coordinator, 3/7/xx   *Tully Panabos*

Employee Name Margaret Montague	Department Information Systems	Date of Report March 7, 19xx

Employee Statement: Please use the space below to describe the incident and how it happened.

At my previous job I frequently worked with a presentation software with which I became very proficient. When I came to TekDyne this software was not on the network, so I brought in a copy I had made while I was at my former job. I installed the copy on the network so that I could do my job better and more efficiently. Several other people asked about the software, and I told them it was on the network. I taught most of the people in the Information Systems Department how to use the software, and everyone was very pleased with the results. Even Mr. Kutner complimented me on the charts I made for him. Now I am being accused of software piracy. I did not know I was doing anything wrong. I thought I was helping TekDyne by sharing this excellent software program. I am sorry that this has happened and assure you that I will never again install copied software on the network.

[X] Check here if you would like to have this incident investigated by a Peer Investigative Panel.

Employee Signature and Date   *Margaret Montague*   3/7/xx

Supervisor Name Gary Santos	Date of Report March 7, 19xx

Supervisor Statement: Please use the space below to comment on the employee statement.

Margaret's statement is correct to the best of my knowledge. I regret that someone did not look into the matter of software licensing when Margaret first installed the software. Margaret has been an outstanding employee during her time with TekDyne, and I would be very sorry to lose her. Her intentions were good, and she did not know she was breaking the law and risking a stiff fine for TekDyne.

Supervisor Recommendation:

I recommend that we purchase a license to use this software immediately and that Margaret's part in this incident be overlooked. After all, she did not know better, and she is an excellent employee.

Supervisor Signature and Date   *Gary Santos*   3/7/xx

Recommendation by Peer Investigative Panel:

Date: March 28, 19xx
To: Help Desk
From: Diem Nhu, Payroll Department
Subject: Printer Problem

The laser printer in the Payroll Department has stopped working. It is displaying a message that says:

52 ERROR

Can you please send someone in to fix it or tell me how to fix it so that I can print paychecks.

Thanks,

Diem

Message	Description
00 READY	The printer is ready to use.
02 WARMING UP	The printer is warming up
20 TONER LOW	Press [Continue] to resume printing. The print quality will begin to degrade as the printer uses the last of the toner in the cartridge. (You can extend the life of a toner cartridge to print a few more pages by removing it from the printer and gently shaking it from side to side.)
25 PRINT OVERRUN	The data sent to the printer were too complex. Press [Continue] to resume printing. You may lose some data. Simplify the page, or use the page protection feature.
38 ERROR	The printer encountered an error while transferring data from the computer. Make sure the printer's serial I/O is set at the same baud rate and parity as the computer. Press [Continue] to clear the error message.
43 ERROR	There is an error in the nonvolatile memory. Press [Continue], then check your control panel settings.
52 ERROR	A temporary error occurred while printing. This error most commonly occurs when the paper selection knob of the universal tray is not set to the size of the installed paper, or when the printer picks two sheets of paper at once. The page containing the error will automatically be printed. Ensure that the paper selection knob is set for the installed paper. Remove the page from the output bin and press [Continue].
58 ERROR	The printer identified a problem while checking its memory. Refer to the Owner's Manual for instructions on clearing this message.
62 ERROR	A temporary error has been detected in the printer. Press [Continue] to resume operation.

Date: March 30, 19xx

To: Help Desk Trainee

From: Ted Kutner, CEO

Subject: Information Resources

I enjoyed the opportunity to see what's happening in Help this week, and I really appreciate the work you did putting together the Metric Conversion Guide and the Electrical Current Prefixes poster. You did an excellent job, and I know the other company personnel will appreciate having this information at their fingertips. I know this will reduce the number of help calls you receive for this routine information.

I have thought of another way to reduce calls from inside personnel, and I think we should do this right away. I would like you to develop a list of resources for basic information, such as:

- Resistor color codes
- Metric electrical quantities, units, and symbols
- Component descriptions and uses
- Printer error codes

Please add any other topics you feel would be helpful.

With this information available in each department, staff won't have to keep calling you for information and you can then focus on the technical details you enjoy.

Trainee Self-Evaluation and Transfer Report

Trainee Name	Team Approval	Date	Chapter 5

Performance Record in Help Desk:

Place a check in the column that best describes your performance in each area:

Area of Training	Outstanding Progress	Shows Improvement	Needs Work
Attitude			
Timeliness of Work			
Attendance/Punctuality			
Accuracy/Thoroughness			
Interest/Team Participation			
Knowledge			
Equipment Proficiency			
Work Habits/Appearance			
Ethics			

Project Points Earned This Department Week 1		
Week 2		Math Proficiency Exam #3

Comments:

Department Transferred To: **Field Services**	Start Date:
Instructor Signature	Trainee Signature

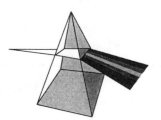

In Basket

Chapter 6
Field Services

TekDyne Guidelines

Position Description and Training Objectives
Field Services Trainee

Department Profile

TekDyne offers on-site repairs and consulting to many customers. Field Services technicians visit the client site, diagnose problems, and make any necessary repairs at the customer's facility. The technicians' trucks are equipped with an inventory of frequently used components, testing equipment, tools, and manuals. In some ways, Field Services is like a traveling repair department that has an additional responsibility for customer relations. Tact and diplomacy, exceptional listening skills, and concern for the customer are essential skills for the Field Services Technician. In addition, the technician must have excellent technical skills to enable each step from troubleshooting and diagnosing a problem to implementing the solution. Trainees in the Field Services Department assist in scheduling site visits, completing work orders, maintaining truck inventories, and participating in team problem solving. Field Services trainees continue to participate in math and achievement training with emphasis on interpersonal skills and financial responsibility.

Objectives

By the end of the Field Services module, trainees will:

- Schedule site visits within prescribed constraints.
- Develop scripts to demonstrate effective and ineffective methods of communication.
- Explain and use algebraic formulas to calculate unknowns.
- Calculate and analyze the impact of distance, time, and speed on payroll and travel expenses.
- Differentiate between relevant and irrelevant information in communication.
- Explain and use work orders to record job completion information.
- Identify and demonstrate employee behavior that supports customer satisfaction.
- Describe career options in the field of technology.
- Describe the financial aid possibilities available to students.
- Calculate the expenses involved in a project.
- Identify the difference between billable rates and pay rates.

Chapter 6 Projects, Field Services	
• Work Orders, pp. 152-155 • 529 Power Supplies, p. 156 • Travel Analysis, pp. 157-158 • Truck Inventories, p. 159 • Travel Reimbursement, p. 160	• Scheduling Example, p. 161-162 • Stormy Day at Fulmune, p. 163 • Schedule #1, p. 164 • Schedule #2, pp. 165-167 • Hank's Wish List, p. 168
Math Proficiency, Field Services	
Exam #4: Algebraic Terms: Roots and Powers	

Module 6-1, Field Services

Trainee: *Your instructor will provide the information necessary to plan your work for the week. Please record this information below for discussion with your team.*

Reading Assignments:

   TekDyne Employee Manual, pages_____

   _____

   _____

Assignments	Due Date	Maximum Points	Special Instructions
TekDyne Employee Manual Assignments			
Additional Assignments			
Total Possible Points This Week:			

Module 6-2, Field Services

Trainee: *Your instructor will provide the information necessary to plan your work for the week. Please record this information below for discussion with your team.*

Reading Assignments:
    TekDyne Employee Manual, pages_____

_____

_____

Assignments	Due Date	Maximum Points	Special Instructions
TekDyne Employee Manual Assignments			
Additional Assignments			
Total Possible Points This Week:			

Module 6-1, Field Services

Team_____   Team Member _____

Performance Expectations: All work is to be thorough, neat, accurate, and completed on time. Teams should assist members in defining outstanding, excellent, satisfactory, and unacceptable performance.

This team member is responsible for completing the following tasks:

Project	Specific Tasks	Special Expectations

Trainee Acceptance of Assignment: I agree to perform the tasks assigned above to the best of my ability and to have my performance on these tasks evaluated constructively by my peers.

Signature: Date:

Team members, please sign below:

_____

_____

_____

Module 6-2, Field Services

Team_____   Team Member _____

Performance Expectations: All work is to be thorough, neat, accurate, and completed on time. Teams should assist members in defining outstanding, excellent, satisfactory, and unacceptable performance.

This team member is responsible for completing the following tasks:

Project	Specific Tasks	Special Expectations

Trainee Acceptance of Assignment: I agree to perform the tasks assigned above to the best of my ability and to have my performance on these tasks evaluated constructively by my peers.

Signature: Date:

Team members, please sign below:

_____

_____

_____

Module 6-1, Field Services

Team _____

Team Worker of the Week
This team member is recognized for outstanding team support and earns a 5% grade bonus.

As a team, evaluate each member on task performance and on group interaction by checking one line in each column. Be certain that the team agrees on the meanings of each level of performance.

Team Member:	Name		Name		Name		Name	
	Task	Group	Task	Group	Task	Group	Task	Group
Outstanding								
Excellent								
Satisfactory								
Needs Improvement								
Limited Progress								

Grade Distribution

This team agrees that members contributed the following percentages of work this week and will earn the following percentage of the portfolio grade (percentages must total 100%).

Percentage:				
Grade: To be completed by instructor				

Self-Assessment

Use one word to describe your overall rating of your own performance this week. Explain any difference between the team evaluation and your self-assessment in the Comments section below.

My Performance:				
Comment on your attitude, timeliness of work, attendance, punctuality, accuracy, thoroughness, interest, knowledge, equipment proficiency, work habits, appearance, ethics.				
Team Member Signatures:				

Employee Development Program   Team Performance Evaluation

Module 6-2, Field Services

Team _____

Team Worker of the Week
This team member is recognized for outstanding team support and earns a 5% grade bonus.

As a team, evaluate each member on task performance and on group interaction by checking one line in each column. Be certain that the team agrees on the meanings of each level of performance.

Team Member:	Name		Name		Name		Name	
	Task	Group	Task	Group	Task	Group	Task	Group
Outstanding								
Excellent								
Satisfactory								
Needs Improvement								
Limited Progress								

Grade Distribution
This team agrees that members contributed the following percentages of work this week and will earn the following percentage of the portfolio grade (percentages must total 100%).

Percentage:				
Grade: To be completed by instructor				

Self-Assessment
Use one word to describe your overall rating of your own performance this week. Explain any difference between the team evaluation and your self-assessment in the Comments section below.

My Performance:				
Comment on your attitude, timeliness of work, attendance, punctuality, accuracy, thoroughness, interest, knowledge, equipment proficiency, work habits, appearance, ethics.				
Team Member Signatures:				

Customer Service Standards

1. The customer is always right.

2. TekDyne customers are valued and important: We serve them.

3. TekDyne tries to please customers. If we fall short, we offer free service for the chance to try again.

4. When customers are served well, we keep their business and gain that of referrals. How we treat them is how we keep them.

5. When customers are not served well, we lose their business and may never have an opportunity to serve their referrals.

6. If we do our jobs well, customers will have no need to complain.

7. If a customer does complain, we listen respectfully, investigate, and resolve the complaint.

8. Goodwill costs little but reaps ample rewards.

9. TekDyne employees recognize and appreciate our customers.

10. Satisfied customers are our business.

Voice Mail Message Transcription

Hi, this is Betty Rodriguez. I think I caught a cold yesterday, so I won't be in today. Since I was running late all day yesterday, I didn't complete my work orders on site. Could somebody please complete them for me today? They are in my locker, which I left unlocked.

My first trip yesterday was to Parson Enterprises. What a trip! Traffic was tied up for miles and it took me two hours just to get there. Once I got there, I spent some time listening to Mr. Parson complain about my slow response time. He was in a really bad mood, so I just let him vent for a while. He says he doesn't like the way the 529 Power Supply problem was handled. I was there from 10:05 until 12:15 and replaced a resistor in the oscilloscope that was not working. It should be okay now. I'll call Mr. Parson next week to follow up.

Next I went to Mitey Mice Products. Boy, have they got problems! They had a lot of rain damage and their carpets were soaking wet. I replaced the potentiometer in their power supply, and it should be okay now. They have a new product that is similar to a remote mouse, but it is a lot faster. Moe Mitey told me that now they are designing a gadget that promises to be a better mouse trap. I was there from 2:00 until 3:00, and I told Moe I would be back next week to replace a bad switch on the oscilloscope.

My final trip of the day was to Wallace Electronics, where I re-tested the power supply I repaired last week. It works fine now, but I don't think they really use it properly. I explained the importance of following the instructions in the user manual and told them to call our Help Desk if they have questions. I was only there from 3:45 to 4:15, but I was glad to be on my way home!

I hope to be back in the truck again tomorrow. Feel free to call me at home if you have any questions—324-9800. Bye!

Customer:	Date:	Work Order Number
Parson Enterprises	April 3, 19xx	431

Description of the Problem:

Oscilloscope not working properly.

Technician:

Betty Rodriguez

Work Completed:

Arrival Time:	Departure Time:

Parts Used:

Follow Up:

Customer:	Date:	Work Order Number
Mitey Mice Products	April 3, 19xx	432

Description of the Problem:

529 power supply working erratically.

Technician:

Betty Rodriguez

Work Completed:

Arrival Time:	Departure Time:

Parts Used:

Follow Up:

TekDyne

Work Order

Customer: Wallace Electronics	Date: April 3, 19xx	Work Order Number 433

Description of the Problem:

Follow up on power supply repairs from last week.

Technician:

Betty Rodriguez

Work Completed:

Arrival Time:	Departure Time:

Parts Used:

Follow Up:

TekDyne

MEMORANDUM

Date: March 27, 19xx

To: Yan Cheng, Field Services Manager

From: Robert Monroe, Repairs Manager

Subject: 529 Power Supplies

After much analysis the repair department has determined that many of the recent problems with the 529 Power Supply are the result of a few bad resistors used in the power supplies built in November and December last year.

Rather than recall all 529s manufactured during that time, the Management Committee has agreed that field technicians will test the questionable resistors at clients' locations. To avoid removing the resistors from the units, technicians will measure the voltage drop across the resistors with the power supply operating.

The desired value of the resistors, the current that should flow through the resistor with the device operating properly, and the actual voltage drop measured across the resistors are shown below.

Use Ohm's law ($V = IR$) to determine if the resistors appear to be within tolerance. (Hint: It may be useful to find the minimum and maximum voltage drop that would be observed if each resistor were within specified tolerance.)

Resistor #102   2.2 KΩ 5% 2.6 mA   measured voltage drop   5.3 V

Resistor #116   680 Ω 1%   15 mA   measured voltage drop   10.4 V

Resistor #149   2.7 KΩ 5% 0.6 mA   measured voltage drop   2.2 V

Date:	April 3, 19xx
To:	Trainee
From:	Yan Cheng
Subject:	Travel Analysis

In a Management Meeting yesterday, Mr. Kutner asked me to analyze travel time and costs for the Field Services Department. He feels that we are spending more time than necessary on the road and are costing the company excessive amounts of money. I think our analysis will show that this is not necessarily true.

I have designed the attached spreadsheet for you to complete. Please fill in all the missing information and return the spreadsheet to me.

Thanks,

Yan

Field Services Department
Month of March, 19xx

Trip	Distance (miles)	Avg Speed (mph)	Trip Time (hours)	Salary at $12 hr	Expense at $.28 per mile	Total Cost
1	40.00	32	1.25	15.00	11.20	26.20
2		43	2.17			
3	207.40		3.40			
4		25	.25			
5	31.50		1.05			
6	43.68	39				
7	115.50		2.10			
8		31	1.42			
9	19.44	27				
10	45.45		1.01			
11		52	1.65			
12	27.06	33				
13	44.16		.96			
14		31	2.20			
15	172.26	54				
16					29.85	54.45
17		37		13.20		24.60
Total						
Avg						

E-MAIL FOR FIELD SERVICE

Date: April 5, 19xx
To: Field Service
From: Peg Nixon, Parts Department
Subject: Truck Inventories

Please help me track some missing inventory information. I would appreciate it if you could write a formula for each of these questions and then perform the calculations. That way I won't have to ask you to help me next time.

Question	Formula and Calculations
1. Completed Work Orders indicate that a technician used 14 battery clips from his truck inventory. To replace these battery clips, the technician requisitioned one-fourth of the mandatory truck inventory. How many battery clips are required in the mandatory truck inventory?	
2. Milly Bright uses 36 switches during an average week. She will be spending the next three weeks visiting client sites in a distant part of the state. To avoid driving back to restock her truck each week, Milly has requisitioned enough switches to get by for three weeks. How many switches does she need?	
3. Mike Louie requisitioned 640 feet of soldering iron in 20-foot rolls. How many rolls of soldering iron does he need?	
4. Casey Shore says that a supply of 36 yellow LED will last him only 3 days. He needs a two-week supply. How many does he need?	
5. Charles Vincent continually loses or misplaces components. He has been warned that future losses would be deducted from his paycheck, and he has agreed to this arrangement. Yesterday he lost a package of 185 resistors worth $.50 each. Charles earns $12 per hour. How many hours must he work to pay for the lost resistors?	
6. Pete Marino requisitioned 800 feet of wire to install a series of antennas for one of our customers. If each antenna requires 150 feet of wire, how many antennas can Pete install?	

Mr. Cheng,

Mr. Kutner recently returned from a trip to Europe where he visited a number of our clients. He has given me his mileage so that I may file his expense report, but the mileage is listed in kilometers. I know the Field Services personnel sometimes travel in Europe, and I am hoping that they can convert these kilometers to miles and calculate the amount ($.28 per mile) to be reimbursed for me.

Thank you very much for your help.

JC

Distance	Miles	Reimbursement
17 km		
139 km		
46 km		
52 km		
785 km		
437 km		
621 km		
760 km		
82 km		
14 km		
542 km		
327 km		
26 km		
4 km		
123 km		
Totals:		

TekDyne

MEMORANDUM

Date: March 30, 19xx

To: Yan Cheng, Field Services Manager

From: Winston Lui, Accounting Manager

Subject: Mileage Expenses

Yan, your department showed a 42 percent increase in mileage expenses last month. With expenses like this it is impossible to budget effectively. What's more, the prices for our products are partially based on the anticipated expense of servicing them; if service expenses increase, then product prices must also increase.

I suspect that some of the technicians have become careless about scheduling. Please remind them that they must calculate mileage between sites and schedule visits in the order that results in the LOWEST POSSIBLE TOTAL MILEAGE. I have attached an example for the technicians to follow and will appreciate your taking care of this problem.

TekDyne Guidelines
Scheduling Site Visits by Mileage

Example

Assume that you picked up your work orders today and found that you had three sites to visit:

- Site A
- Site B
- Site C

Along with the work orders, the scheduling clerk gave you a map showing distances between the three client sites and TekDyne:

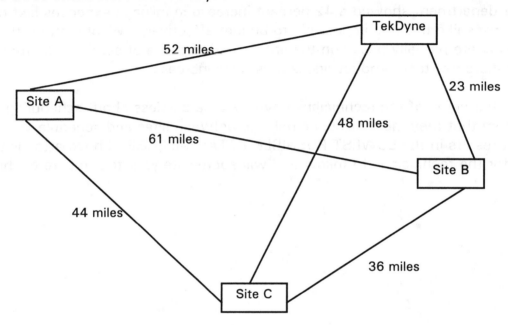

Consider the possible routes and calculate the mileage for each:

Home to A to B to C to Home 52 + 61 + 36 + 48 = 197	Home to A to C to B to Home
Home to B to C to A to Home	Home to B to A to C to Home
Home to C to A to B to Home	Home to C to B to A to Home

1) Select and circle the route with the lowest total mileage.
2) At average speeds of 40 mph and using the lowest mileage, how many hours will the technician spend traveling? _____
3) At average speeds of 40 mph and using the highest mileage, how many hours will the technician spend traveling? _____
4) At $.28 per mile, what is the total travel expense using the lowest mileage? _____
5) At $.28 per mile, what is the total travel expense using the highest mileage? _____
6) At $12 per hour, (lowest mileage), how much is the technician paid for time he is traveling? _____
7) At $12 per hour, (highest mileage) how much is the technician paid for time he is traveling? _____

Stormy Day at Fulmune

Today has been an especially difficult day. Your first site visit was to Cranston Enterprises, where you responded to an emergency situation that ended up taking longer to repair than you had expected. As you started up the truck to head for your next site, Fulmune Electronics, you tried to phone Fulmune to let them know you were running late; but your cell phone was not working

Thunder and lightning and heavy sheets of rain and hail slowed traffic on the freeway to barely a crawl, causing you to be even later. When you finally arrived at Fulmune (five hours later than planned), Pete Fulmune really let you have it. He had worked himself into a storm to equal the one outside, and he let you know it. Pete complained that without working equipment he was unable to serve his own customers, and that if he lost customers because of TekDyne's slow service he would never buy TekDyne equipment again.

After listening to Pete complain, you made your way to the broken equipment. This particular piece of equipment connects to a computer that runs on Windows 95. It became immediately apparent to you that the problem was not with the TekDyne equipment, but rather with the computer. You recognized the problem because Fulmune had called you to repair the same problem on two other occasions. You also knew how to correct the problem because of your expertise in computer hardware and software. However, it isn't your responsibility to fix equipment that is not manufactured by TekDyne.

What's more, the problem is a direct result of Pete Fulmune's carelessness. You told him on both previous occasions that he must exit from all programs before turning the computer off. He just doesn't seem to believe it. Since Pete created his own problem, you are tempted to tell him to fix it himself— especially after the unpleasant reception he gave you today! Then you think about how angry Pete already is and how this latest information is going to affect him.

Here he comes now. What are you going to do and say?

Sites to Visit: Merriwether, Inc.   Hydratech
                   Louis Electronics   Prentiss Co.
                   Fairchild Industries   Jasper Electronics

Mileage Estimates:

List sites in schedule order:

1. TekDyne
2. _____
3. _____
4. _____
5. _____
6. _____
7. _____
8. TekDyne

Total Mileage: _____

Trainees, remember that Mr. Lui wants us to schedule trips for minimum mileage. Don't worry about anything else.

Yan

TekDyne

MEMORANDUM

Date: April 4, 19xx

To: Yan Cheng, Field Services Manager

From: Winston Lui, Accounting Manager

Subject: Scheduling

Yan, I appreciate the effort your department has made to reduce travel costs, and you have done a fine job of doing just that. However, I may have been hasty in asking that you schedule sites by mileage only. I understand we have had a number of calls from upset customers because of increased response time. As you know, we guarantee 24-hour response time—regardless of the mileage involved.

In the future, please schedule site visits with the following in mind:

- Minimize response time
- Minimize mileage
- Minimize overtime

Of course, you should also take into consideration the amount of time to be spent at each site, time spent en route, truck inventories and parts availability, and urgency of repairs.

Today's Date: April 4, 19xx

Customer	Date Called In	Time Called In	Estimated Visit Time
Merriwether, Inc.	April 3	10:00 a.m.	30 minutes
Louis Electronics	April 3	11:30 a.m.	1 hour
Fairchild Industries	April 3	1:00 p.m.	1 hour
Hydratech	April 3	1:05 p.m.	2 hours
Prentiss Company	April 3	3:00 p.m.	1 hour
Jasper Electronics	April 3	5:30 p.m.	30 minutes

Assume average travel speeds of 40 mph.
Assume sufficient supplies and equipment are in stock on the truck.
Estimated mileage is shown on the next page.
Assume departure from TekDyne at 8 a.m. and return to TekDyne only after completing all stops.

Worksheet

Miles	Customer	Arrival Time	Departure Time

Mileage Estimates:

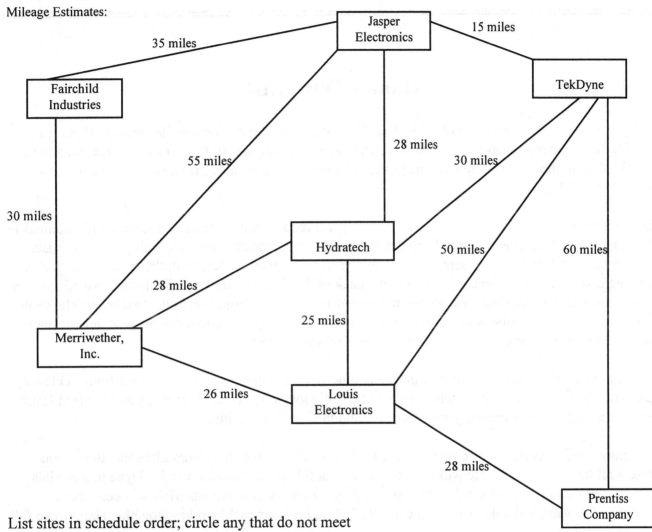

List sites in schedule order; circle any that do not meet guaranteed response time:

1. TekDyne
2. _____, arrival time _____
3. _____, arrival time _____
4. _____, arrival time _____
5. _____, arrival time _____
6. _____, arrival time _____
7. _____, arrival time _____
8. TekDyne, arrival time _____

Total Mileage: _____

ON THE JOB SITUATION #4

Hank's Wish List

Today you had an interesting lunch with Hank Carlson, the owner of Carlson Electronics. Hank grew up with Ted Kutner and has been a long-time customer of TekDyne. Both Carlson and TekDyne have benefitted from the relationship over the years, but sometimes it seems as if Hank expects a little too much from TekDyne.

Hank has taken on an ambitious new project which will require construction of a series of 12 antennas in the lot next to the Carlson facility. Each antenna will be mounted atop a 68-foot-tall pole. The posts will be spaced 5 feet apart in a semi-circle, with the first one placed 3 feet from the front of the Carlson building and the last one placed 3 feet from the back of the Carlson building. Cable will extend from the front of the Carlson building through conduit buried 15 inches underground to the first pole. The cable will then be run up the first pole, across the tops of the other 11 poles, down the last pole, and through conduit 15 inches underground to the back of the Carlson building.

Hank suggested that since he will be purchasing much of the equipment for this project from TekDyne, TekDyne should construct the antennas as a gesture of good will. As lunch ended, you promised Hank that you would talk it over with your supervisor and then get back to him.

You know from experience that your supervisor, Yan Cheng, will only discuss ideas like this if you present all the information. He will want to know what this project would cost TekDyne in materials and labor. You know that the cable will cost $4.32 per foot. Additional materials will cost about $275.00. The work will take two technicians (at $22.00 per hour each) working together about three full days to complete.

How much will the total project cost?

What will you recommend to Mr. Cheng?

TekDyne

MEMORANDUM

Date: April 4, 19xx

To: All Field Service Personnel

From: Ted Kutner, CEO

Subject: Quality

Most of you are aware that for every hour you spend in a customer's facility that customer is billed $115.00. At that price, they expect only the highest quality. In most cases, we give them a level of service that is priceless.

I received a call from one customer last week who commented on the quality of our organization, and I wanted to pass his compliment on to those of you who earned it. This customer, for whom we logged 58 billable hours last year, told me that when a TekDyne technician is in his facility the technician's pleasant attitude and cheerful disposition are contagious. He also told me that the professional appearance of our technicians makes a positive influence on his employees. This customer said that TekDyne technicians are worth every penny he pays for billable hours.

Thank you, Field Services personnel, for earning this fine compliment.

Notes

Trainee Self-Evaluation and Transfer Report

Trainee Name	Team Approval	Date	Chapter
			6

Performance Record in Field Services:

Place a check in the column that best describes your performance in each area:

Area of Training	Outstanding Progress	Shows Improvement	Needs Work
Attitude			
Timeliness of Work			
Attendance/Punctuality			
Accuracy/Thoroughness			
Interest/Team Participation			
Knowledge			
Equipment Proficiency			
Work Habits/Appearance			
Ethics			

Project Points Earned This Department   Week 1

Week 2   **Math Proficiency Exam #4**

Comments:

Department Transferred To: **Engineering and Design**	Start Date:
Instructor Signature	Trainee Signature

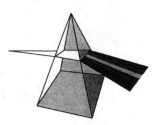

TekDyne
Creating Tomorrow's Solutions Today

One TekDyne Circle, Livermore, CA 94123

In Basket

Chapter 7
Engineering and Design

TekDyne Guidelines

Position Description and Training Objectives
Engineering and Design Trainee

Department Profile

TekDyne operates in a dynamic and highly competitive industry. To underwrite its success in this environment, the company takes an aggressive approach to product development. The team of technicians and engineers in this department work closely with Sales and Marketing to brainstorm, research, and analyze market needs. They then design a new product, identify the components involved, build a prototype, and analyze costs. Trainees in this department participate in new product review and selection, cost and price analysis, initial marketing plans, and development of the sales presentation. Trainees continue the Human Resources achievement training, with emphasis on conflict resolution and lifelong learning.

Objectives

By the end of the Engineering and Design module, trainees will:

- Review and evaluate suggested new products.

- Analyze production costs for a new product.

- Determine selling price for a new product.

- Present a preliminary marketing plan and description of the new product.

- Develop scripts to demonstrate effective methods of conflict resolution.

- Solve problems using various forms of Ohm's law.

- Solve problems that contain both real and literal numbers.

- Assemble and test a sound-activated switch.

- Define a potential project in which the sound-activated switch could be used.

Chapter 7 Projects, Engineering and Design
• New Product Review, p. 178
Math Proficiency, Engineering and Design
No math proficiency exam in this department

Module 7, Engineering and Design

Trainee: *Your instructor will provide the information necessary to plan your work for the week. Please record this information below for discussion with your team.*

Reading Assignments:

TekDyne Employee Manual, pages_____

_____

_____

Assignments	Due Date	Maximum Points	Special Instructions
TekDyne Employee Manual Assignments			
Additional Assignments			
Total Possible Points This Week:			

Module 7, Engineering and Design

Team_____   Team Member _____

Performance Expectations: All work is to be thorough, neat, accurate, and completed on time. Teams should assist members in defining outstanding, excellent, satisfactory, and unacceptable performance.

This team member is responsible for completing the following tasks:

Project	Specific Tasks	Special Expectations

Trainee Acceptance of Assignment: I agree to perform the tasks assigned above to the best of my ability and to have my performance on these tasks evaluated constructively by my peers.

Signature: Date:

Team members, please sign below:

_____

_____

_____

Employee Development Program   Team Performance Evaluation

Module 7, Engineering and Design

Team _____

Team Worker of the Week
This team member is recognized for outstanding team support and earns a 5% grade bonus.

As a team, evaluate each member on task performance and on group interaction by checking one line in each column. Be certain that the team agrees on the meanings of each level of performance.

Team Member:	Name		Name		Name		Name	
	Task	Group	Task	Group	Task	Group	Task	Group
Outstanding								
Excellent								
Satisfactory								
Needs Improvement								
Limited Progress								

Grade Distribution
This team agrees that members contributed the following percentages of work this week and will earn the following percentage of the portfolio grade (percentages must total 100%).

Percentage:				
Grade: To be completed by instructor				

Self-Assessment
Use one word to describe your overall rating of your own performance this week. Explain any difference between the team evaluation and your self-assessment in the Comments section below.

My Performance:				
Comment on your attitude, timeliness of work, attendance, punctuality, accuracy, thoroughness, interest, knowledge, equipment proficiency, work habits, appearance, ethics.				
Team Member Signatures:				

TekDyne

MEMORANDUM

Date: April 12, 19xx

To: Trainees

From: Dallas Fenton, Engineering and Design Manager

Subject: New Product Review

Welcome to Engineering and Design! I have heard glowing reports of your success in the other TekDyne departments, and I look forward to working with you. I hope you will be as excited about the work we do here as the rest of us are.

I want to get you started right away, so I have arranged for some product designers to present their suggested projects to you today and tomorrow. Be sure to take notes on the projects they demonstrate, and ask any questions you like. By tomorrow you will have to choose one of the projects for the company to adopt. Here is the procedure:

1. Identify the components in the product and price them. Use a spreadsheet to develop a total materials cost.

2. Estimate the labor costs associated with the product.

3. Estimate the number of units to be manufactured and sold over the next year.

4. Establish a selling price based on a reasonable markup.

5. Present the product to the company. Include all of the above information and reasons why TekDyne should adopt this new product.

Good luck!

Trainee Self-Evaluation and Transfer Report

Trainee Name	Team Approval	Date	Chapter 7

Performance Record in Engineering and Design:

Place a check in the column that best describes your performance in each area:

Area of Training	Outstanding Progress	Shows Improvement	Needs Work
Attitude			
Timeliness of Work			
Attendance/Punctuality			
Accuracy/Thoroughness			
Interest/Team Participation			
Knowledge			
Equipment Proficiency			
Work Habits/Appearance			
Ethics			

Project Points Earned This Department Week 1			
Week 2	NA	Math Proficiency Exam	NA

Comments:

Department Transferred To: **Human Resources**	Start Date:
Instructor Signature	Trainee Signature

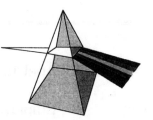

In Basket

Chapter 8
Human Resources

TekDyne

MEMORANDUM

Date: April 15, 19xx

To: Employee Development Program Graduates

From: Christine Bennett, Human Resources Manager

Subject: Exit Interview

Welcome back to Human Resources! It has been a pleasure to observe your progression through the TekDyne Employee Development program. The final exercise in the program allows you an opportunity to express your opinions and to make suggestions and recommendations based on what you have learned about TekDyne as an organization and about yourself as a trainee.

Please team with another trainee and conduct the Exit Interview you will find on the next page. You should interview each other and note brief responses to each of the questions. When you have completed the interview, your TekDyne training program will be complete.

Good luck and best wishes for a successful and fulfilling career in technology.

Name	Date

In which area do you feel training helped you improve most:
     Attitude
     Effort
     Team Participation
     Attention to Detail
	Comments:

Which was your favorite department?	Which was your least favorite department?
What was the most challenging project?	What was the most rewarding project?
Which project was the most surprising?	Which was the most enjoyable project?
Which major area of study will you pursue?	What type of company would you like to work for?
Additional comments:	
Interviewed by:	

TekDyne
MEMORANDUM

Date: April 15, 19xx

To: Trainees

From: Ted Kutner, CEO

Subject: Employee Recognition

Congratulations on having completed your training program with TekDyne. By now you are aware of not only the functions of our various departments, but also our mission, our approach to customer service, and our appreciation of our excellent employees. I think it is particularly appropriate that you should complete your training on Employee Recognition Day.

Your assistance as a trainee has been highly valued by the department managers. I hope for an opportunity to work with you on many projects and events as time progresses. Meanwhile, please accept my sincere best wishes for a successful and rewarding career.